TREASURE ISLAND

Written by Robert Louis Stevenson

Teacher Guide

MEMORIA PRESS
www.MemoriaPress.com

TREASURE ISLAND
Written by Robert Louis Stevenson
TEACHER GUIDE
Contributing Editors: Cheryl Lowe, Jennifer Farrior, and Sean Brooks

ISBN 978-1-61538-071-8

Cover illustration by Starr Steinbach

Contents

Treasure Island

Teaching Guidelines	4
Introduction	6
Chapter 1 & Chapter 2	8
Chapter 3	10
Chapter 4	12
Chapter 5	14
Chapter 6	16
Mastery Word Review (Ch. 1-6)	18
Chapter 7	20
Chapter 8	22
Chapter 9	24
Chapter 10	26
Chapter 11	28
Mastery Word Review (Ch. 7-11)	30
Chapter 12	32
Chapter 13	34
Chapter 14	36
Chapter 15	38
Chapter 16	40
Mastery Word Review (Ch. 12-16)	42
Chapter 17 & Chapter 18	44
Chapter 19	46
Chapter 20 & Chapter 21	48
Chapter 22	50
Chapter 23 & Chapter 24	52
Mastery Word Review (Ch. 17-24)	54
Chapter 25	56
Chapter 26	58
Chapter 27	60
Chapter 28	62
Chapter 29	64
Mastery Word Review (Ch. 25-29)	66
Chapter 30	68
Chapter 31	70
Chapter 32	72
Chapter 33	74
Chapter 34	76
Mastery Word Review (Ch. 30-34)	78

Appendix of Nautical Terms

General Terms	82
Labeled Diagram of Ship	86
Parts of a Ship	87
Sails and Parts of Sails	87
Boats and Ships	88
Ropes and Knots	88
Wind and Sea, Directions, and Sailing Terms	89

Discussion Questions Key

Chapters 1-11	92
Chapters 12-19	93
Chapters 25-33	94

Quizzes & Final Test 95

Quizzes & Final Test Key 111

PREPARING TO READ:

REVIEW

- Orally review any previous vocabulary.
- Review the plot of the book as read so far.
- Periodically review the concepts of character, setting, and plot.

STUDY GUIDE PREVIEW

- Reading Notes:
  - Read aloud together.
  - This section gives the student key characters, places, and terms that are relevant to a particular time period, etc.
- Vocabulary:
  - Read aloud together so that students will recognize words when they come across them in their reading.
- Comprehension Questions:
  - Read through these questions with students to encourage purposeful reading.

READING:

- Student reads the chapter (or selection of the chapter for that lesson) independently or to the teacher (for younger students).
- For younger students, you can alternate between teacher-read and student-read passages. Model good reading skills. Encourage students to read expressively and smoothly. Teacher may occasionally take oral reading grades.
- While reading, mark each vocabulary word as you come across it.
- Have students take note in their study guide margin of pages where a comprehension question is answered.

AFTER READING:

VOCABULARY

- Look at each word within the context that it is used, and help your student come up with the best synonym that defines the word. (Make sure it is a synonym the student knows the meaning of.)
- Record the word's meaning in the students' study guides. (Use students' knowledge of Latin and other vocabulary to decipher meanings.)

COMPREHENSION QUESTIONS

- Older students can answer these questions independently, but younger students (2nd-4th) need to answer the questions orally, form a good sentence, and then write it down, using correct punctuation, capitalization, and spelling. (You may want to write the sentence down for the younger student after forming it orally, and then let the student copy it perfectly.)
- It is not necessary to write the answer to every question. Some may be better answered orally.
- Answering questions and composing answers is a valuable learning activity. Questions require students to think; writing a concise answer is a good composition exercise.

QUOTATIONS AND DISCUSSION QUESTIONS

- Use the Quotations and Discussion Questions section of each lesson as a guide to your oral discussion of the key concepts in the chapter that may not be covered in the Comprehension Questions.
- These talking points can take your oral discussion to a higher level than covered in the students' written work. Use this time as an opportunity to introduce higher-level thinking. You can introduce concepts the students may not be mature enough to fully understand yet but that would be beneficial for them to begin thinking about.
- A key to the Discussion Questions is in the back of the Teacher Guide.

ENRICHMENT

- The Enrichment activities include composition, copywork, dictation, research, mapping, drawing, poetry work, literary terms, and more.
- This section has a variety of activities in it, but the most valuable activity is composition. Your student should complete at least one composition assignment each week. Proof student's work and have student copy composition until grammatically perfect. Insist on clear, concise writing. For younger students, start with 2-3 sentences, and do the assignment together. The student can form good sentences orally as you write them down, and then the student copies them.
- These activities can be completed as time and interest allow. Do not feel you need to complete all of these activities. Choose the ones that you feel are the best use of your students' time.

UNIT REVIEW AND TESTS

- There is a unit review and a quiz or test following every few lessons (varies by individual guide).
- On the weeks that have these reviews and tests, you may want to do the review early in the week, and then drill it orally a couple of times before giving the test at the end of the week.
- A final comprehensive test is also included.

Introduction: Robert Louis Stevenson

Robert Louis Stevenson (1850-1894) was born in Edinburgh, Scotland. Although Stevenson suffered from tuberculosis, which caused his early death at age forty-four, he did not let his physical weaknesses hinder him from living an adventurous life.

As he was often bed-ridden with his illness, Stevenson began at an early age to entertain himself by making up stories.

This passion for creating a world apart from his own did not stop as he entered his adult life, despite his family's attempt to discourage him. In 1867 he entered the University of Edinburgh to study engineering, for his family's profession was lighthouse design. However, he had no desire for his studies, and spent more energy in creating friendships with his fellow students.

In 1871 Stevenson announced to his father that he was not fit to be an engineer and would pursue life as a writer.

He gained inspiration for his stories as he traveled around the world, despite uncomfortable and even dangerous means, and risking his health besides. His adventures included pursuing his future wife halfway around the world, being suspected as a spy by the French police, and immersing himself in the culture of the South Pacific islands, amongst what most people of the time would have called savage cannibals.

When *Treasure Island* was published in the 1880s, it was extremely popular among children and adults alike. Even in Stevenson's time, pirates were not at all common, so he decided to set his story during the 1700s, and used strange words to give the story an older feel.

After battling sickness and depression later in life, Stevenson bounced back to write what he felt was his best work, *Weir of Hermiston*; however, he died before he could complete it.

While Stevenson was wildly popular in his day, the rise of modern literature after the first World War lowered his reputation to a second-class writer, and he suffered criticism by other notable literary figures, such as Virginia Woolf. Regardless, Stevenson has been admired by Ernest Hemingway, Rudyard Kipling, and G. K. Chesterton, among many others.

To this day, Stevenson remains very popular, and is ranked the 25th most translated author in the world, ahead of fellow nineteenth-century writers Charles Dickens, Oscar Wilde, and Edgar Allan Poe.

Some of Stevenson's other works include *Kidnapped, A Child's Garden of Verses*, and *The Strange Case of Dr. Jekyll and Mr. Hyde.*

Robert Louis Stevenson is an example of how following your true passion, despite sickness, opposition, and criticism, can truly be rewarding. And we are rewarded with the opportunity to partake in swashbuckling adventure in the fantastic world he created within the pages of *Treasure Island.*

Reading Notes

Jim Hawkins	the narrator of the story; young boy
Dr. Livesey	the doctor who tends to Jim's father; confronts the captain
Admirable Benbow	the name of the inn that Jim's father runs
the captain/Billy Bones	the old seaman with a scar on his cheek who lodges at the inn
Black Dog	a seaman missing two fingers; looking for Bill at the inn

Vocabulary

Write the meaning of each bold word or phrase.

1. the **sabre** cut across one cheek, a dirty, **livid** white n. sword … adj. discolored
2. he drank slowly, like a **connoisseur*** n. expert
3. seemed like a **mate** or **skipper** n. ordinary sailor … n. a sea captain
4. a thousand **diabolical** expressions adj. devilish, evil
5. wringing his hands after such a **rebuff** n. a blunt or abrupt rejection
6. the **ruffian** had told him n. a tough, lawless person
7. if it's only for a piece of **incivility** like tonight's n. rudeness, misbehavior
8. a pale, **tallowy** creature adj. waxy
9. half **fawning**, half **sneering** v. showing extreme affection … v. smirking
10. exposed his great **sinewy** arm adj. muscular
11. *Look up the following words in the dictionary and write out the complete definition, the alternate forms, and 2-3 synonyms for each word:

    connoisseur- n. a specialist in a given field whose opinion is highly valued

    alternate forms: connoisseurship- n.

    synonyms: expert, judge, specialist, aficionado, arbiter

*Teachers: Vocabulary words with an asterisk are Mastery Words and will appear in the quizzes.

Comprehension Questions

Answer the following in complete sentences.

1. What does the captain ask Jim to do for him? How much does he pay Jim for this?

   The captain asks Jim to keep his "weather-eye open for a seafaring man with one leg" and let him know as soon as he appears. The captain gives Jim a silver fourpenny once a month for this duty.

2. What haunts Jim's dreams? Describe these dreams. *The seafaring man with one leg haunts Jim's dreams. He sees him in a thousand different forms with a thousand different expressions. In each dream the leg is cut off at different places, and sometimes Jim is even chased by this man.

3. Contrast Dr. Livesey and the captain. Why is Dr. Livesey able to humiliate the captain who had terrorized everyone else? Where is Dr. Livesey mentioned before this encounter? Dr. Livesey is "neat" and "bright" with snow white skin and "bright, black eyes and pleasant manners," while the captain is a "filthy, heavy, bleared scarecrow of a pirate," drunk on rum, with poor manners. The doctor remains calm and steady when he addresses the captain, and is not threatened by him. Dr. Livesey is mentioned at the beginning of the novel as being one of the people to ask the narrator to record everything that had happened to him.

4. Why does Black Dog come to the inn, and what is the captain's reaction to him? *Black Dog comes to the inn in search of the captain to be paid a debt. The captain is surprised to see Black Dog, and looks old and sick at the sight of him.

5. What happens between Black Dog and the captain when Jim leaves the room? When Jim leaves the room, Black Dog and the captain begin talking, then yelling, and then the captain attacks Black Dog with his cutlass, and they both come running out.

*Teachers: Comprehension Question answers with an asterisk indicate important plot points that will appear in the quizzes.

Quotations

Identify the speaker of the following.

"I'm a plain man; rum and bacon and eggs is what I want." the captain

"Silence, there, between decks!" the captain

"Ah, Bill, Bill, we have seen a sight of times, us two ..." Black Dog (to the captain)

"If it comes to swinging, swing all, say I." the captain (to Black Dog)

"I clear my conscience—the name of rum for you is death." Dr. Livesey (to the captain)

Discussion Questions

1. Describe the old seaman. Does he fit the description of a pirate? Why or why not?
2. Why do you think this particular dream keeps haunting Jim? Have you ever been haunted by something in a dream?
3. Would you call Black Dog and the captain friends? Why or why not?
4. What was Dr. Livesey's advice to the captain? Do you agree with this advice?

Reading Notes

the blind beggar the man who delivers the black spot to the captain; walks with a stick

Vocabulary

Write the meaning of each bold word or phrase.

1. That's a **summons**, mate. n. a demand to surrender; an authoritative command
2. He **clambered** up and down stairs v. climbed with effort or difficulty
3. his temper was more **flighty** adj. unpredictably excitable, unstable
4. gripped it in a moment like a **vice** n. a clamp used to hold something in position
5. It **cowed** me more than the pain. v. intimidated; frightened with a show of force
6. The captain had been struck dead by thundering **apoplexy**. n. a stroke

Comprehension Questions

Answer the following in complete sentences.

1. How does the captain get Jim to bring him some rum? What does he ask Jim to do for him if he can't "get away nohow"? The captain tries to bribe Jim, but reminding him that the doctor said one glass wouldn't hurt him is what persuades Jim to get the rum. The captain asks Jim to tell the doctor to signal or summon the magistrates ("pipe all hands") to the Admiral Benbow Inn.
2. What keeps Jim busy and distracts him from worrying about the captain? The death of Jim's father, funeral preparations, neighborly visits, and the work at the inn keep Jim busy and distracted from worrying about the captain's health and his orders.
3. Describe the captain's behavior as he grows sicker. As he grows sicker, the captain becomes weaker, "clamber[ing] up and down the stairs," holding onto the walls for support as he walks, and breathes hard and fast. His temper is more flighty and violent. When he is drunk he will draw his cutlass and lay it on the table. He bothers people less and is more quiet.

4. Who comes to visit the captain? Describe him. A blind beggar comes to visit the captain. He walks with a stick, wears a green shade over his face, hunches over, and wears a tattered cloak with a hood. He is a very "dreadful-looking" figure.

5. How does the captain react to this visitor? What happens between them? The captain is shocked into sobriety upon seeing the blind beggar. "The expression of his face was not so much of terror as of mortal sickness." The blind beggar passes something from his hand to the captain's. As soon as he passes the note off, the blind beggar is gone in a hurry.

6. What is Jim's reaction to the captain's collapse? Jim runs to the captain at once, calling his mother. When he realizes the captain is dead, he bursts into tears. "It was the second death I had known, and the sorrow of the first was still fresh in my heart."
(*You'll need to know the ultimate reason for the captain's death is the shock caused by the black spot.)

Quotations

Identify the speaker of the following.

"Doctors is all swabs." the captain (swab = worthless person)

"Now, if I can't get away nohow, and they tip me the black spot …" the captain

"Take me in straight, or I'll break your arm." the blind beggar (to Jim)

"If I can't see, I can hear a finger stirring." the blind beggar

Discussion Questions

1. What is "the black spot"?
2. What does the captain mean when he says rum has been "meat and drink, and man and wife" to him?

Reading Notes

Captain Flint the name that carried a great weight of terror with the people

Vocabulary

Write the meaning of each bold word or phrase.

1. that **detestable** blind beggar adj. intensely disliked, despicable
2. They say cowardice is **infectious**; but then argument is, on the other hand, a great **emboldener**.
   adj. contagious … n. one who gives courage, motivator
3. overcoming a strong **repugnance*** n. disgust, revulsion
4. under that, the **miscellany** began n. a mixture of different items
5. I'll show these **rogues** that I'm an honest woman. n. dishonest people, scoundrels
6. **obstinately** unwilling adv. in a stubborn, unyielding manner

*Look up "repugnance" and "repugnant" in the dictionary and write out the complete definition, the alternate forms, and 2-3 synonyms for each word: n. 1. extreme aversion, repulsion
2. inconsistency or incompatibility of ideas
adj. 1. arousing disgust; extremely distasteful 2. contradictory, conflicting
alternate forms: repugnantly- adv.
synonyms: repulsive, disgusting, abhorrent, off-putting, offensive, nauseating

Comprehension Questions

Answer the following in complete sentences.

1. What do Jim and his mother immediately do after Jim tells his mother all that he knows about the captain? Immediately after Jim tells his mother everything, they run from the inn to the nearest hamlet to ask for help.

2. Describe the reaction of the people in the neighboring hamlet to their situation. The people in the neighboring hamlet are not willing to return to the inn with Jim and his mother; they are afraid of the name of Captain Flint. They give Jim a loaded pistol, say they will have horses waiting for him upon their return, and send a boy to the doctor's for armed assistance.

3. What is Jim's mother's response to them? *Jim's mother tells the townspeople that she and Jim will return to the inn and break open the captain's sea-chest and take what is due them. She calls them "big, hulking, chicken-hearted men."

4. What does Jim find when he searches the captain's body for the key to the chest?
Jim finds the scrap of paper the blind beggar handed him with the black spot on it. He also finds in his pockets small coins, a thimble, thread and needles, a piece of tobacco, his knife, pocket compass, and a tinder box. He then finds the key around the captain's neck after his mother suggests he look there.

5. What does the fact that the captain collected seashells from West India tell us about him?
The West Indian seashells found in the captain's chest tell us that although he was a thieving pirate, he had an appreciation for beauty and the sentimentality to collect mementos from his travels.

Quotations

Identify the speaker of the following.

"Back we will go, the way we came, and small thanks to you big, hulking, chicken-hearted men."
Jim's mother (to the townspeople)

"He had till ten, mother." Jim (about the captain, after reading the note)

"I'll have my dues, and not a farthing over." Jim's mother (farthing = something of very small value)

"And I'll take this to square the count." Jim (referring to the oilskin packet)

Discussion Questions

1. Why does Jim call his mother both "honest and greedy"? Do you agree with him?

Enrichment

1. Research and write a report on the various types of coins found in the captain's sea-chest: *doubloons*, *louis-d'ors*, *guineas*, and *pieces of eight*.

Reading Notes

Pew	the blind beggar
Dirk	one of Pew's men, whom he calls a fool and a coward
Supervisor Dance	police officer who arrives to investigate

Vocabulary

Write the meaning of each bold word or phrase.

1. the **formidable*** beggar adj. intimidating
2. **Rout** the house out! v. to tear apart in search
3. the rest stood **irresolute** on the road adj. hesitant, undecided
4. you stand there **malingering** v. pretending or exaggerating incapacity or illness, so as to avoid duty or work
5. the blind **miscreant*** n. a vicious or depraved person; villain
6. she still continued to **deplore** the balance v. to regret deeply or strongly; lament

*Look up "formidable" in the dictionary, and write out the complete definition, the alternate forms, and 2-3 synonyms.

adj. 1. causing fear or awe; commanding respect

2. difficult to overcome *alternate forms:* formidableness - n. formidably - adv.

synonyms: intimidating, impressive, threatening, dangerous, dreadful, awesome

miscreant- n. & adj. n. a vile or depraved person; a villain

alternate forms: adj. lacking in conscience or moral principles, villainous

synonyms: corrupt, depraved, wicked, criminal, vicious

Comprehension Questions

Answer the following in complete sentences.

1. What does Jim see when he looks back at the inn? Jim sees seven or eight men running towards the inn. Three of the men run together, and the middle man is the blind beggar.

2. Pew and his men don't care about Captain Bones' money. What motivates them to find his chest? *The men are concerned with finding "Flint's fist" (the oilskin packet), something of greater value than mere money.

3. Who else, according to Pew's last words, is involved in the plot? *Black Dog

4. What happens to Pew at the end of the chapter? Pew is left behind by his comrades when the police arrive at the inn. He steps in the path of a horse and is trampled to death.

5. What does Jim find when he goes back to the inn? What does he think about this? Jim finds the inn in a "state of smash." Although nothing besides the captain's money-bag and some money from the cash register have been taken, Jim sees at once that they are ruined, meaning they won't be able to carry on business at the inn.

6. What does Jim tell Supervisor Dance? Jim tells Supervisor Dance that he believes he has what the men were looking for in his breast-pocket and that he wants to put it somewhere safe.

Quotations

Identify the speaker of the following.

"Budge, you skulk!" Pew

"Oh, shiver my soul, if I had eyes!" Pew

"If you had the pluck of a weevil in a biscuit you would catch them still." Pew (pluck = resolution, courage)

"I'm glad I trod on Master Pew's corns." Supervisor Dance

"I believe I have the thing in my breast-pocket." Jim

Discussion Questions

1. What do you think would have happened if the officers had not arrived when they did?
2. What is "Flint's fist"?

Enrichment

1. Draw a picture of the inn after Pew and his men ransack it.

Reading Notes

Squire Trelawney landowner who finances the treasure hunt

Vocabulary

Write the meaning of each bold word or phrase.

1. a **bluff**, rough-and-ready face adj. rough and blunt, but not unkind
2. says he, very stately and **condescending*** adj. patronizing, disdainful
3. close-cropped, black **poll** n. head, scalp
4. This lad Hawkins is a **trump**, I perceive. n. a fine person
5. The Spaniards were so **prodigiously** afraid of him adv. extraordinarily
6. But you are so **confoundedly** hot-headed adv. perplexingly

*Look up "condescend" in the dictionary and write out the complete definition, the alternate forms, and 2-3 synonyms: v. 1. to come down from a superior position 2. to treat someone as inferior; talk down to someone

alternate forms: condescending- adj. condescendingly- adv.

synonyms: 1. humble oneself, stoop, vouchsafe 2. belittle, disdain, patronize

Comprehension Questions

Answer the following in complete sentences.

1. Dr. Livesey and the squire discuss Flint and his treasure. What do they know about Flint?
   The squire has heard of Flint before. He calls him "the bloodthirstiest buccaneer that sailed." He says the Spaniards are extremely afraid of him, and sailors will change course to avoid crossing his path.

2. Describe what is inside Flint's oilskin packet. *The oilskin packet contains a book and a sealed paper. The book is filled with entries of Flint's plunders. The record lasts about 20 years. The paper contains a map of an island, with directions to where the treasure is hidden.

3. Describe the squire's proposed treasure hunt. How is Jim to be included? The squire suggests the doctor give up his practice, while he will go to Bristol for ten days to acquire the best ship with the best crew for the treasure hunt. He believes the trip will involve favorable winds, a quick passage, and not the least difficulty in finding the treasure. He suggests Jim come along as their cabin-boy.

4. What makes Dr. Livesey hesitant to join the treasure hunt? Why?
 *Dr. Livesey is hesitant to join the treasure hunt because of the squire's loud mouth. He feels the squire will not be able to keep the mission a secret, allowing the other pirates to attack them and take the map.

5. What is the squire's response to Dr. Livesey's fear?
 The squire's response to the doctor's fear is, "I'll be as silent as the grave."

Quotations

Identify the speaker of the following.

"Hawkins has earned better than cold pie." Trelawney

"Heard of him! Heard of him, you say!" Trelawney (about Flint)

"Thrifty man! He wasn't the one to be cheated." Dr. Livesey (about Flint)

"I'll be as silent as the grave." Trelawney

Discussion Questions

1. What do you think about the squire's attitude regarding the treasure hunt?
2. Do you believe what the squire says in response to Dr. Livesey's fear? Why or why not?

Enrichment

1. Bury or hide something in your backyard or house. Then draw a map leading to its location, including landmarks, such as trees or furniture. Have a parent or friend try to find your "treasure" using your map.

Mastery Word List

condescend **connoisseur** **formidable** **miscreant** **repugnance**

Synonym Substitution

Write a few good synonyms or a phrase in the blank to replace the highlighted word.

1. The massive army stood **formidably** just to their west. threateningly, imposingly, dangerously, intimidatingly
2. Stop that **miscreant** before he escapes! criminal, delinquent, felon
3. "Fortune has rarely **condescended** to be the companion of genius." - Isaac Disraeli
   come down, conceded, humbled itself, stooped
4. It turns out his sister is a far more **formidable** opponent than he originally anticipated.
   threatening, imposing, dangerous, impressive, powerful
5. You could say that when it comes to chocolate cake I am a **connoisseur**.
   expert, appreciator, fan, specialist
6. The strange child found pizza to be quite **repugnant**. bad, offensive, disgusting
7. A **condescending** boss is rarely respected. arrogant, patronizing, disdainful
8. His report was **repugnant** to the information he originally gave.
   inconsistent, contradictory, incompatible

Mastery Substitution

Use a word from the Mastery Word List to replace the highlighted word or phrase.
You may have to change the form of the word to fit the sentence.

1. It doesn't take an **expert** to differentiate between cherry and apple pie. connoisseur
2. "Never yield to force; never yield to the apparently **overwhelming** might of the enemy." - Winston Churchill formidable
3. After the boy told on his brother and sister to their parents, his siblings treated him like a horrible **villain** for the rest of the day. miscreant
4. After he received his grade report, he started speaking **in a manner of superiority** to everyone in the house. condescendingly
5. Judy was overwhelmed with **disgust** when she saw the rat. repugnance
6. Even with all his weapons, nobody would consider Charlie an **intimidating** foe. formidable
7. At the nice Italian restaurant, Dad tried to talk fancy about the menu to make himself look like a **person who knows a lot about Italian food**. connoisseur
8. She was so short that everyone had to **bend down** just to talk to her. condescend

Implementation

Use at least three of the words from the Mastery Word List in a paragraph of your own.

Reading Notes

Tom Redruth	the elderly gamekeeper at the Hall, temporarily in charge of Jim
Hispaniola	the name of the ship Trelawney bought for the expedition
Blandly	an old friend of Trelawney's who sold him a ship; joins the crew

Vocabulary

Write the meaning of each bold word or phrase.

1. I **brooded*** by the hour v. pondered
2. the most **transparent calumnies** n. clearly false and malicious statements
3. wanted a good **berth** as cook n. job, position
4. the most **indomitable** spirit adj. unconquerable, unable to be subdued
5. a **woman of color** n. African American
6. a **capital** imitation of a sailor's walk adj. excellent or first-rate (colloquial)

*Look up "brood" in the dictionary and write out the complete definition, the alternate forms, and 2-3 synonyms: n. the young of certain animals; v. 1. to think or dwell upon moodily and at length 2. keep eggs warm to make them hatch

alternate forms: broodingly- adv. *synonyms*: n. group, children; v. 1. agonized, ruminated, contemplated 2. incubate, nurture n. young, group, flock

Comprehension Questions

Answer the following in complete sentences.

1. Where does Jim stay while waiting for the treasure hunt preparations to be completed? How does he pass the time? Jim stays at the Hall under the charge of Redruth, the gamekeeper. Jim passes the time by daydreaming about islands and adventures, and brooding over the details of the map.

2. What about Trelawney's letter worries Jim? *When Trelawney mentions telling others about the treasure, Jim becomes worried that the doctor will be upset that he hasn't kept his mouth shut as he promised.

3. How did Trelawney find his crew in Bristol? What makes you think the squire was gullible?
Trelawney found many willing to join him on the hunt for treasure. He purchased the ship from Blandly, who joined his crew, and then he met Silver and hired him to be the cook. Blandly and Silver then recruited others for the crew. The squire seems gullible because he trusted what any man told him about themselves, and didn't believe what the townspeople said of them, such as that Blandly will do anything for money.

4. What makes Jim think about the home that he is leaving? How does he react to this?
*When Jim returns home to his mother to find that she has hired an apprentice boy to help her, he realizes that the boy is there to take his place while he is gone. Jim cries over this, then proceeds to treat the apprentice horribly.

5. What is one of Jim's last thoughts before leaving home? One of Jim's last thoughts is of the old captain, "who had so often strode along the beach with his cocked hat, his sabre-cut cheek, and his old brass telescope."

6. What delights Jim upon his arrival to Bristol? When Jim arrives in Bristol, he is delighted by the smell of tar and salt, the many different ships, and by all the old sailors singing and working. "Though I had lived by the shore all my life, I seemed never to have been near the sea till then."

Quotations

Identify the speaker of the following.

"The squire has been talking, after all." Jim

"A pretty rum go if squire ain't to talk for Dr. Livesey, I should think." Redruth

"Imagine the abominable age we live in!" Squire Trelawney

"Sail! We sail tomorrow!" Squire Trelawney

Discussion Questions

1. What qualities would you look for in crew members if you were in the squire's position?
2. What does Trelawney mean when he describes Long John Silver as "a man of substance"?
3. Do you agree with how Jim treats the apprentice boy? What would you have done differently?

Enrichment

1. Draw a picture of the Hispaniola, the schooner (definition in the index) bought by the squire.

Reading Notes

Long John Silver the tall, strong, one-legged sailor hired as a cook for the crew
Tom Morgan an old sailor who was drinking with Black Dog in the tavern
Spy-Glass the tavern where Jim meets Long John Silver

Vocabulary

Write the meaning of each bold word or phrase.

1. he managed with wonderful **dexterity***. n. agility of hand or mind
2. then, **relinquishing** my hand v. giving up, abandoning
3. came forward pretty sheepishly, rolling his **quid** n. a lump of chewing tobacco
4. we laughed together, **peal** after peal n. any loud, sustained sound or series of sounds
5. I was again obliged to join him in his **mirth***. n. merriment, amusement, laughter
6. telling me some little **anecdote** of ships n. a short account of an incident; story

*Look up the following words in the dictionary and write out the complete definition, the alternate forms, and 2-3 synonyms for each word:

dexterity: n. mental or manual skill
alternate forms: dexterous- adj dexterously- adv. dexterousness- n.
synonyms: aptitude, ability, finesse, ingenuity, skill, adroitness, mastery

mirth: n. great enjoyment, merriment
alternate forms: mirthful - adj. mirthfulness - n. mirthfully - adv.
synonyms: amusement, cheer, happiness, levity, pleasure

Comprehension Questions

Answer the following in complete sentences.

1. Describe Jim's meeting with Long John Silver. Give references to Silver and his character.
Jim goes to the Spy-Glass tavern to meet Silver. Silver is immediately pleased to meet Jim, and everything about him sets Jim at ease. He thinks of him as a "clean and pleasant-tempered landlord." Silver shakes Jim's hand upon meeting him, and whispers confidentially to him as though they are old friends, which flatters Jim.

2. Who did Jim originally fear Long John Silver might be?

After reading the squire's letter, Jim was afraid that Silver would prove to be the one-legged sailor that Billy Bones had warned him about, the one that had haunted his dreams.

3. What pirate does Jim see in the Spy-Glass? What is Silver's reaction?

Jim sees Black Dog in the Spy-Glass. He leaves the tavern without paying his bill, and Silver gets very upset. He sends a couple men to chase after him, but they return saying they lost him in the crowd. Silver also questions the man who was talking with Black Dog, Tom Morgan.

4. What is Jim's opinion of Long John Silver?

*After seeing Black Dog, Jim was suspicious of Silver, but Silver's character wins Jim over. "… I would have gone bail for the innocence of Long John Silver." Jim is "comfortable" with Long John.

5. What is the reaction of Dr. Livesey and Squire Trelawney to Silver's story?

Dr. Livesey and Squire Trelawney are upset that Black Dog has gotten away, but they believe nothing more can be done, and that Silver has done his best.

Quotations

Identify the speaker of the following.

But he was too deep, and too ready, and too clever for me. Jim (about Silver)

"You're as smart as paint." Long John Silver (to Jim)

"Why, shiver my timbers." Long John Silver

"The man's a perfect trump." Squire Trelawney (about Silver)

Discussion Questions

1. Are you surprised that Jim so easily trusts Long John Silver? Why or why not?
2. Why do you think Jim says Silver is "one of the best possible shipmates"?

Reading Notes

Captain Smollet	sharp-looking captain of the Hispaniola; disliked by the squire
Arrow	the ship's mate; brown old sailor; friends with the squire

Vocabulary

Write the meaning of each bold word or phrase.

1. All **shipshape** and **seaworthy**? adj. neat, orderly … adj. fit for a sea voyage
2. I was **engaged**, sir, on what we call **sealed orders** adj. employed … n. orders given to a commander of a vessel to be opened after the vessel is out of contact with the shore
3. Now, treasure is **ticklish** work. adj. difficult or risky; tricky
4. But the **slight***, if there be one, was unintentional. n. failure to show respect, discourtesy
5. make a **garrison** of the stern part of the ship n. a body of troops stationed in a fortified place
6. In other words, you fear a **mutiny**. n. revolt or rebellion against an authority

*Look up "slight" in the dictionary and write out the complete definition, the alternate forms, and 2-3 synonyms: adj. 1. small, weak, inadequate 2. slender v. treat or speak of with disdain or neglect n. an act of neglect or discourtesy

alternate forms: slightingly- adv. slightish- adj. slightly- adv. slightness- n.

synonyms: adj- minor, negligible, insignificant v.-disregard, offend, insult, ignore n. affront, disrespect

Comprehension Questions

Answer the following in complete sentences.

1. What are Captain Smollett's complaints? "I don't like this cruise; I don't like the men; I don't like my officer." He doesn't like the fact that the mission is for treasure, and that everyone knows more about it than he does.
2. Compare the reactions of Squire Trelawney and Dr. Livesey to the captain's complaints. *Trelawney does not care for the captain at all, and would have seen him "to the deuce" when he comes to express his complaints, but Dr. Livesey is willing to listen and to address each matter individually to seek out a solution. Afterwards, Dr. Livesey says he feels that the captain and Silver are the only two honest men on board, while Trelawney heartily disagrees with him about the captain, saying he is an "intolerable humbug" and "unmanly, unsailorly, and downright un-English."

3. What does Captain Smollett request? Is this done?

Captain Smollett requests the ship be organized and prepared for combat, and that the information regarding the island, map, and treasure be kept confidential from the crew. Yes, these requests are obliged immediately.

4. How does Jim feel about the captain? Why?

Jim agrees with the squire and hates the captain "deeply." Jim feels this way in part because the captain makes him get to work, and tells the doctor, "I'll have no favorites on my ship."

Quotations

Identify the speaker of the following.

"Well, sir, better speak plain … I don't like this cruise; I don't like the men; and I don't like my officer. That's short and sweet." Captain Smollett

"… I'll tell you my way of it—life or death, and a close run." Captain Smollett

"Contrary to all my notions, I believe you have managed to get two honest men on board with you—that man and John Silver." Dr. Livesey

"… as for that intolerable humbug, I declare I think his conduct unmanly, unsailorly, and downright un-English."

Trelawney (about Captain Smollett)

Discussion Questions

1. Do you agree with Squire Trelawney or Dr. Livesey in regard to Captain Smollett? Why?

Enrichment

1. Read Aesop's fable "A Mountain in Labor." Copy this fable onto another piece of paper, and write a paragraph explaining what Dr. Livesey means when he compares Captain Smollett's errand and misgivings to it.

   The moral of this fable is: much ado about nothing. Dr. Livesey believes that Captain Smollett is making too big a deal out of the circumstances.

Reading Notes

Job Anderson	the boatswain who takes over as mate after Arrow disappears
Israel Hands	the coxswain; experienced seaman; confidant of Silver
Barbecue	the crew's nickname for Long John Silver

Vocabulary

Write the meaning of each bold word or phrase.

1. And then the whole crew **bore** chorus v. to bring forth (past tense of *bear*)
2. he began to appear on deck with **hazy** eye adj. confused, misty, thick with haze
3. he carried his crutch by a **lanyard** round his neck n. a short rope used in rigging
4. I seen him **grapple*** four v. to seize in a grip, take hold of
5. the dishes hanging up **burnished** adj. polished, brightened
6. the last day of our outward voyage, by the largest **computation** n. calculation

*Look up "grapple" in the dictionary and write out the complete definition, the alternate forms, and 2-3 synonyms. v. & n. v. 1. to seize and hold firmly 2. to ponder and evaluate a problem 3. to wrestle or fight n. 1. iron claw attached to a rope, used for boarding enemy ships 2. a close hand-to-hand struggle *alternate forms:* grappler - n. *synonyms:* v. 1. grip, clasp, hold 2. struggle with 3. fight, scuffle, skirmish

Comprehension Questions

Answer the following in complete sentences.

1. What carries Jim back to the Admiral Benbow "in a second"? Why? Hearing the sailors' song reminds Jim of the Admiral Benbow Inn because that was the song Captain Bones often sang there.

2. Describe Mr. Arrow's character. What happens to him? *Mr. Arrow is always drunk, has no authority with the crew, and often hurts himself or lies in bed all day. One night he just disappears and is seen no more; the captain believes he fell overboard, and is not very disappointed by it.

3. How does Long John Silver move about on the ship? What is the general opinion of him by the crew? What does the coxswain tell Jim about Silver? Silver carries his crutch around his neck to free up his hands, and uses lines across the ship to make his way about. He is able to move just as quickly as the other men. The whole crew respects and obeys Silver, for he is very friendly and does everybody some kind of service. The coxswain tells Jim that Silver is "no common man" and that he is educated, brave, and strong.

4. Does Captain Smollett have a change of heart regarding his original complaints? Explain. *Captain Smollett admits he was wrong about the crew, and that they are brisk and well behaved. He even comes to really fancy the ship itself. However, he still claims to dislike the cruise.

5. How does the apple barrel prove to be significant? The apple barrel proves to be significant because it is where Jim ends up overhearing an important conversation.

Quotations

Identify the speaker of the following.

"He's no common man, Barbecue." the coxswain/Israel Hands (to Jim about Silver)

"Pieces of eight! pieces of eight! pieces of eight!" Silver's parrot (named Cap'n Flint)

"She'll lie a point nearer the wind than a man has a right to expect of his own married wife, sir."

Captain Smollett (about the ship)

"A trifle more of that man, and I should explode." Trelawney (about Captain Smollett)

Discussion Questions

1. What does Silver mean when he says, "You can't touch pitch and not be mucked"?

Enrichment

1. Find on a world map the places that Silver's parrot has traveled: Madagascar, Malabar, the Surinam, Providence, Portobello, and Goa.
2. Find the definitions of the following nautical terms: *coxswain* (in index), *grog*, *duff*, *the trades* (in index), *bowsprit* (in index), *helm* (in index), *luff* (in index).

grog: liquor … *duff*: a stiff flour pudding boiled in a bag

Reading Notes

Dick the crew's youngest hand; Jim overhears him speaking with Silver

Vocabulary

Write the meaning of each bold word or phrase.

1. asked Silver, **derisively*** adv. mockingly
2. Dick's **square.** adj. just, fair, or honest, faithful
3. you was a kind of a **chapling**, John n. chaplain, a person who says the prayer at an assembly
4. Put 'em ashore like **maroons**? n. people who are abandoned on a desolate island
5. Don't you get sucking of that **bilge**, John. n. lowest part of a ship; also the foulness which collects there
6. You fill a **pannikin** and bring it up. n. a small pan or metal cup

*Look up "derisive" in the dictionary and write out the complete definition, the alternate forms, and 2-3 synonyms: adj. expressing or deserving ridicule or mocking

alternate forms: derisively- adv. derisiveness- n.

synonyms: ridiculing, mocking, taunting, sarcastic

Comprehension Questions

Answer the following in complete sentences.

1. Who does Jim overhear talking while he's in the apple barrel? What are they discussing?
   Jim overhears Long John Silver talking to Dick, a young seaman. The coxswain, Israel Hands, soon joins them. They are discussing their plan to keep the treasure for themselves after it is found.
2. What is said that hurts Jim's feelings? What is his reaction to this? Jim is hurt when Silver tells Dick he is "as smart as paint" in exactly the same words he told to Jim. Jim is so upset that, if he were able, he would kill Silver through the barrel.
3. What becomes clear about Silver's relationship to Pew and Flint? Silver tells Dick that he, Pew, and Flint were all on the same crew, and that he, Silver, was the most frightening of all of them. Many of Flint's old crew is here on board now.

4. What is Silver's plan? Silver's plan is to allow Captain Smollett to sail the ship safely to the island, allow the squire and the doctor to locate the treasure using the map, load it onto the ship, and then get rid of all of them.

5. What does Dick question about the plan? What is Silver's response? Why? *Dick asks Silver what is to be done with the crew after their cruise is thwarted. Silver admires Dick for asking this question because it shows that he is thinking everything through. Silver replies that they must be killed because he doesn't want them coming back somehow to ruin his good fortune.

6. What is Silver's one request about the plan? *Silver's one request is that he kill Trelawney himself.

7. How does Jim know that there are still innocent men on board? When Jim hears the coxswain whisper to the cook that nobody else after Dick will join them in their plan, he knows there are still some faithful men on board the ship.

Quotations

Identify the speaker of the following.

"But now, you look here: you're young, you are, but you're as smart as paint. I see that when I set my eyes on you, and I'll talk to you like a man." Silver (to Dick)

"I didn't half a quarter like my job till I had this talk with you, John; but there's my hand on it now." Dick

"You'll have your mouthful of rum tomorrow, and go hang." Silver (about the crew)

"Dooty is dooty, mates. I give my vote—death." Silver

Discussion Questions

1. What is a "gentleman of fortune"?
2. What does the phrase "Dead men don't bite" mean?
   This question will also appear in Chapter 29's Enrichment section, if not completed here.

Enrichment

1. Draw a picture of the scene with Jim in the apple barrel. Include details.
2. Silver mentions "Execution Dock." Research what he is referencing.

Mastery Word List

brood	**derisive**	**dexterity/**	**grapple**
mirth	**slight**	**dexterous**	

Synonym Substitution

Write a few good synonyms or a phrase in the blank to replace the highlighted word.

1. When the servant did not bow, the master took it as a great **slight**. offense, matter of disrespect, insult
2. Very few people are equally **dexterous** with both hands. agile, skillful, able
3. "Teach us to delight in simple things, and **mirth** that has no bitter springs." - Rudyard Kipling
   joy, merriment, laughter
4. The child **grappled** with the desire to get out of her chair.
   fought, wrestled, dealt
5. After the death of Patroclus, Achilles **brooded** over how he would get his revenge.
   thought over, deliberated, agonized
6. The bad movie earned many **derisive** comments from the viewers.
   mocking, disdainful, sarcastic
7. The musician demonstrated his **dexterity** on multiple instruments. skill, ability
8. "No amount of ability is of the **slightest** avail without honor." - Andrew Carnegie
   smallest, minutest, tiniest
9. He simply couldn't **grapple** with the idea that Santa Claus may not be real.
   think about, deal with, ponder
10. The children looked **derisively** at the bunny pajamas they received from their grandmother.
    disdainfully, mockingly, scoffingly, contemptuously
11. "Black are the **brooding** clouds and troubled the deep waters." - Charles Dickens
    gloomy, worrying, discouraging
12. He **slighted** his duties, being constantly distracted by the thought of a swim in the pond.
    neglected, treated as unimportant, ignored

Mastery Substitution

Use a word from the Mastery Word List to replace the highlighted word or phrase.
You may have to change the form of the word to fit the sentence.

1. It doesn't help to **dwell** on a bad grade. brood
2. The speech was so **deserving of ridicule** that the speaker was booed by the audience.
derisive
3. He greets everyone he meets with great **joy and excitement**. mirth
4. The party was completely **without any laughter or merriment**, and people soon started to leave.
mirthless
5. After their fight, Judy would intentionally **ignore** Katy when they passed in the hall.
slight
6. While he was searching the cave, Henry discovered a **family** of vipers.
brood
7. It takes a lot of **skill and agility** to climb a mountain. dexterity
8. His nervous laughter made them think he was speaking to them **in a mocking manner.**
derisively
9. Even though she was much older, her mind was as **capable** as it ever was. dexterous
10. No one enjoys being **treated as unimportant** by his friends. slighted

Implementation

Use at least three of the words from the Mastery Word List in a paragraph of your own.

Reading Notes

Skeleton Island — the name of the land in sight; a main place for pirates at one time
Spy-glass — the main hill on the island, where the pirates kept a look-out
Capt. Kidd's Anchorage — the name of the anchorage on the island

Vocabulary

Write the meaning of each bold word or phrase.

1. There all hands were already **congregated**. v. assembled, gathered
2. if such was your intention as to enter and **careen** v. to tilt over
3. the **coolness** with which John **avowed** his knowledge n. composure; calm … v. confessed
4. I had … taken such a **horror** of his cruelty, **duplicity***, and power n. feeling of loathing and fear; strong dislike … n. deceitfulness in speech or conduct
5. then make some **pretence** to send for me n. deception; false appearance
6. The doctor changed **countenance** a little n. appearance, esp. the look or expression of the face

*Look up "duplicity" in the dictionary, and write out the complete definition, the alternate forms, and 2-3 synonyms.

n. intentional deceptiveness; double-dealing
alternate forms: duplicitous - adj.
synonyms: cunning, deceit, fraud, treachery, betrayal

Comprehension Questions

Answer the following in complete sentences.

1. How does Jim know that Silver will be disappointed by the map the captain pulls out?
By the fresh look of the map, Jim knows it is not the same map they had found in Bones' chest.

2. What surprises Jim about Silver? *Jim is surprised by John's coolness when giving information about the island. He is still in amazement at his deceptive nature, how he can seem to be nice outwardly, but inwardly be plotting their murder.

3. After Jim tells the squire, the doctor, and the captain about what he overheard, what do they immediately do? After hearing Jim's tale, the men immediately make Jim sit down at the table, pour him a glass of wine, and fill his hands with raisins. Each of them bows to Jim, drinking to his good health, and their service to him, for his luck and courage.

4. What is each of their responses to this news? The squire immediately apologizes to the captain, admitting he was wrong, and awaits his orders. The captain also apologizes, believing he should have seen the signs of a mutiny. The doctor tells the captain he believes that Silver had fooled them all. The squire is also outraged at such behavior from so-called Englishmen, and he feels he could find it in his heart to blow up the ship.

5. What are the captain's three points? The captain's three points are 1) they have to continue on the journey, because the crew would rise up at once if he ordered them to turn around, 2) they still have a little time left, until the treasure is found, and 3) there are still faithful hands on board, so they still have a chance at surviving the battle.

6. How do the men feel about Jim's role in this situation? How does Jim feel about this? Why? *They believe Jim can help them more than anyone else, because the crew is open with him. They all have faith in him. Jim is intimidated by this because he feels "altogether helpless." He feels they are greatly outnumbered; the grown men on their side is 6 to the others' 19.

Quotations

Identify the speaker of the following.

"He'd look remarkably well from a yard-arm, sir." Captain Smollett (about Silver)

"You, sir, are the captain. It is for you to speak." Trelawney (to Captain Smollett)

"And to think that they're all Englishmen! Sir, I could find it in my heart to blow the ship up." Trelawney

"Hawkins, I put prodigious faith in you." Trelawney

Discussion Questions

1. What does the captain mean when he says Silver would "look remarkably well from a yard-arm"?
2. How would you feel if you were in Jim's position at the end of the chapter?

Vocabulary

Write the meaning of each bold word or phrase.

1. The Spy-glass … was likewise the strangest in **configuration** n. an arrangement of parts in a particular form or figure
2. the whole ship creaking, groaning, and jumping like a **manufactory** n. factory
3. I never learned to stand without a **qualm*** or so n. uneasy feeling; apprehension
4. A peculiar **stagnant** smell hung over the anchorage adj. stale or foul from standing
5. the birds once more flying and **squalling** around the anchorage v. screaming or crying loudly and harshly
6. It is one thing to be idle and **skulk** v. to shirk duty; to malinger

*Look up "qualm" in the dictionary, and write out the complete definition, the alternate forms, and 2-3 synonyms. n. 1. a momentary sick feeling 2. a prick of the conscience 3. an uneasy feeling of apprehension or doubt *alternate forms:* qualmish - adj. *synonyms:* uncertainty, hesitation, queasiness, concern; scruple, compunction

Comprehension Questions

Answer the following in complete sentences.

1. Describe the island. The island is entirely land-locked, buried in woods, the shores mostly flat, and the hill-tops standing round at a distance … two little rivers, two swamps, emptying into a pond … the foliage around the shore has a kind of poisonous brightness … not a breath of air moving, nor a sound … a peculiar stagnant smell hangs over the anchorage.
2. The crew is ready to mutiny. What does the captain have in mind when he says Silver is their "one man to rely on"? What advantage does Silver have in keeping the peace? *The captain says Silver is their one man to rely on because he is clearly the leader of the mutinous crew and still believes the doctor, squire, captain, and Jim are ignorant of his plan. The captain believes Silver wants to end the mutiny and smooth things over to avoid a fight, so he wants to give him that chance, making the men as "mild as lambs."

3. What is the crew's reaction after the captain suggests they go ashore? What is behind Captain Smollett's decision not to protest?

After the captain suggests the crew go ashore, they come out of their skulks immediately and give a cheer. Captain Smollett immediately gets out of the way, leaving Silver to arrange the party. Jim comments that it is a good thing he was not there, as it would have been impossible not to understand the situation—Silver is now the captain of a rebellious crew.

4. What is Jim's spontaneous decision? Does he regret it? Explain why or why not. Jim decides to sneak onto one of the boats going ashore with the crew. At first he regrets this decision when Silver notices him in the boat. But we know that Jim looks back on this decision with no regret because he states it is the "first of the mad notions that contributed so much to save [their] lives."

Quotations

Identify the speaker of the following.

"I don't know about treasure, but I'll stake my wig there's fever here." Dr. Livesey

"Is that you, Jim? Keep your head down." the bow oar

"Jim, Jim!" Silver (after he spots Jim in the boat)

Discussion Questions

1. The doctor says he smells fever on the island, and the whole crew seems to have caught the "infection" of mutiny. Why does the author so closely use the analogies of fever and infection when referring to Treasure Island?
2. Do you like or dislike the fact that occasionally Jim informs the reader about the ultimate outcomes of his decisions? Why or why not?

Enrichment

1. Draw a picture of Jim in the boat heading to the island.
2. Find the definitions of the following nautical terms: *scupper*, *boom* (in index), *block*, *warp*, *pike*, *gig* (in index).

   scupper: a drain or spout allowing water on the deck to flow overboard … *block*: pulley … *warp*: to move by hauling on a line that is fastened to or around an anchor or pier … *pike*: long spear

Reading Notes

Tom the honest seaman; killed by Silver

Alan another honest seaman; screams out when killed by the mutineers

Vocabulary

Write the meaning of each bold word or phrase.

1. an open piece of **undulating**, sandy country v. moving with a wavelike motion
2. raising my head to an **aperture** among the leaves n. an opening, as a hole, gap, etc.
3. disturbed the **languor** of the afternoon n. lack of energy or vitality; sluggishness
4. Tom lay motionless upon the **sward**. n. grassy land; meadow
5. several **modulated** blasts adj. varying in pitch or tone
6. Instantly I began to **extricate*** myself and crawl back v. to free or release from entanglement; to disengage

*Look up "extricate" in the dictionary, and write out the complete definition, the alternate forms, and 2-3 synonyms. v. to loosen or set free from difficulty or constraint

alternate forms: extricable - adj. extrication - n.

synonyms: release, liberate, rescue, deliver, free, extract

Comprehension Questions

Answer the following in complete sentences.

1. What is Jim's initial emotion after escaping into the island? Why? *Initially Jim feels the "joy of exploration." He enjoys discovering the different types of plants, rivers, and animals on the island, such as a rattlesnake.
2. Who does Jim overhear conversing? What are they saying? Jim overhears John Silver and an honest seaman from the crew named Tom. Tom is confronting Silver about the mutiny, while Silver is trying to convince Tom to join them, in order to save his life.
3. What interrupts this conversation? The conversation is interrupted by a man's cry, scream, "death-yell."

4. What follows as a result from this conversation? *When Tom questions Silver about this yell, Silver admits that it was Alan who has just been killed, another honest seaman from the crew. Tom is outraged and challenges Silver to kill him as well. He turns to walk off, but Silver stabs him in the back with a branch, breaking his back. Then Silver stabs him twice, killing him.

5. What is Jim's reaction to this turn of events? Explain in detail. Jim is horrified, and he almost faints. Jim now thinks of Silver as a "monster." "I could scarce persuade myself that murder had been actually done, and a human life cruelly cut short a moment since, before my eyes." He's in shock.

Quotations

Identify the speaker of the following.

"If I hadn't took to you like pitch, do you think I'd have been here a-warning of you?"
Silver (to Tom)

"It's a black conscience that can make you feared of me." Tom (to Silver)

"Then rest his soul for a true seaman!" Tom (about Alan)

"If I die like a dog, I'll die in my duty." Tom

Discussion Questions

1. To which animals does the author/Jim compare Silver? What other words are used in the place of Silver's name, labeling him? What effect does this have on the reader?

Enrichment

1. Research rattlesnakes. Write a short paper on their physical characteristics, habitat, eating habits, and why they are so dangerous.

Reading Notes

Ben Gunn marooned on the island for three years; former member of Flint's crew

Vocabulary

Write the meaning of each bold word or phrase.

1. The terror of this new **apparition** brought me to a stand n. anything that appears, esp. something remarkable or startling
2. behind me the murderers, before me this lurking **nondescript**. n. a person or a thing of no particular or notable type or kind
3. a system of the most various and **incongruous** fastenings adj. not harmonious in character; lacking harmony of parts
4. brass buttons, bits of stick, and loops of **tarry gaskin** n. loose breeches smeared with tar, or like tar
5. leather belt, which was the one thing solid in his whole **accoutrement**. n. personal clothing
6. the cannon-shot was followed … by a **volley** of small arms n. the simultaneous discharge of a number of missiles or firearms

Comprehension Questions

Answer the following in complete sentences.

1. What is it that makes Silver appear "less terrible" to Jim? Why? The "lurking nondescript" that Jim sees but cannot identify makes Silver less terrible to him. He prefers the dangers that he knows to those he does not. This man turns out to be Ben Gunn.
2. Who is Ben Gunn? Describe him. Ben Gunn is a man that was left behind on the island by his crew three years previously. He is a white man, his skin burned by the sun. He has black lips and fair eyes. He is the "chief for raggedness" among all the beggars Jim has seen. His clothes are made from tatters from an old ship's canvas and sea cloth.
3. Why does Ben Gunn want to come with Jim on board the ship? *Ben Gunn wants to come aboard with Jim for some "Christian" food, mainly cheese. He also wants a ride home and one thousand pounds of money, which he feels is rightly his anyway.

4. What connects Ben Gunn with Silver and the treasure? Ben was part of Flint's crew when he buried the treasure on the island. Flint went out with six other men to bury the treasure, but he came back alone, the other six dead and buried. Among the other men left on the crew were Silver and Billy Bones. Later, Ben arrived at the island with another crew and told them of the treasure buried there. They searched for twelve days before leaving Ben behind, telling him he could find Flint's money for himself.
   **Ben Gunn credits Providence for putting him on the island.

5. What does Ben Gunn tell Jim to say about him to the others? Ben tells Jim to tell the others on board that he is a good and pious man and that he puts more confidence in a gentleman born than a gentleman of fortune.

Quotations

Identify the speaker of the following.

"If ever I can get aboard again, you shall have cheese by the stone." Jim (to Ben Gunn)

"You'll bless your stars, you will, you was the first that found me!" Ben Gunn (to Jim)

"If you was sent by Long John, I'm as good as pork, and I know it." Ben Gunn (to Jim)

"Now, I'll tell you what. So much I'll tell you, and no more. I were in Flint's ship when he buried the treasure." Ben Gunn (to Jim)

Discussion Questions

1. Ben Gunn believes that Providence put him there on the island. What does he mean by this? Do you agree with him?
2. What do you think Ben Gunn means when he says he puts more confidence in a gentleman born than a gentleman of fortune?

Enrichment

1. Ben Gunn refers to the game of "chuck-farthen." Find out how to play this game, then play it with your classmates.
2. When Ben Gunn says to Jim, "You're all in a clove hitch, ain't you?" he's metaphorically referring to a type of knot. Research this knot. Then find a piece of rope, and see if you can tie it yourself.

Reading Notes

John Hunter	one of Squire Trelawney's men
Richard Joyce	one of Squire Trelawney's men
Abraham Gray	one of the ship's crew; joins up with the captain and his men

Vocabulary

Write the meaning of each bold word or phrase.

1. If ever a man smelt fever and **dysentery**, it was in that abominable anchorage. n. inflammatory disorder of the lower intestinal tract, resulting in pain, fever, and diarrhea
2. it was in that **abominable** anchorage adj. detestable; dreadful; atrocious
3. in the direction of the **stockade** upon the chart. n. defensive structure consisting of walls or mounds built around a stronghold to strengthen it
4. the thing was completed by a **paling** six feet high n. picket fence
5. they might have held the place against a **regiment**. n. army, legion, battalion
6. tossed our stores over the **palisade**. n. fence; enclosure

Comprehension Questions

Answer the following in complete sentences.

1. What makes the doctor's pulse go "dot and carry one" (skip a beat)? Why? When the doctor hears Alan's death cry, his heart skips a beat. He is scared because he thinks the cry came from Jim and that he is now dead.
2. Why is the doctor not worried about going back to the ship for a second load of provisions? Why do they dump the remainder of the weapons and ammunition overboard? The doctor knows the mutineers have the advantage of numbers, but he and his men have the advantage of arms. They dump the rest of the arms and powder overboard so the mutineers cannot use it against them.
3. Describe how Smollett handles Gray. *Smollett singles Gray out among the six mutineers and requests that he join their party. He tells Gray he believes he is a good man deep down. He also points out that he (Smollett) is risking his life and the lives of others to wait on Gray to join them.

4. How does Captain Smollett discover Gray's loyalty? After Smollett's request, there is a scuffle below, and Gray appears with a knife-cut along one cheek. He then says, "I'm with you, sir," showing his loyalty.

5. Why is Smollett so anxious to bring Gray ashore? Smollett is anxious to bring Gray with them because they need all the men they can get on their side, and he wants to be able to defend the stockade before they lose it to the mutineers on the island.

Quotations

Identify the speaker of the following.

"There's a man … new to this work. He came nigh-hand fainting, doctor, when he heard the cry. Another touch of the rudder and that man would join us." Smollett (about one of the forecastle hands)

"I know you are a good man at bottom, and I daresay not one of the lot of you's as bad as he makes out." Smollett (to Gray)

"I'm risking my life, and the lives of these good gentlemen, every second." Smollett (to Gray)

"I'm with you, sir." Gray (to Smollett)

Discussion Questions

1. Why does the author switch the narrative to the doctor's perspective in this chapter? Is this confusing or interesting? Explain.
2. What does the incident between Smollett and Gray further reveal about Smollett's character?

Enrichment

1. Research the system of bells used during the sailors' watches. In the first line of this chapter, the doctor says, "It was about half past one—three bells in the sea phrase." How much time has gone by on the watch?
2. Draw a picture of the stockade, using the details given in the chapter.

Mastery Word List

duplicity **extricate** **formidable** **grapple**

mirth **qualm**

Synonym Substitution

Write a few good synonyms or a phrase in the blank to replace the highlighted word.

1. It turns out his sister is a far more **formidable** opponent than he originally anticipated.
   threatening, imposing, dangerous, impressive, powerful
2. The tax collector had no **qualms** with taking a little extra money off the top.
   problems, moral reservations, shame, reluctance
3. It is difficult to find many lawyers who are not **duplicitous** with their words.
   dishonest, deceitful, devious, smooth
4. "Teach us to delight in simple things, and **mirth** that has no bitter springs." - Rudyard Kipling
   joy, merriment, laughter
5. The dog barked relentlessly until he was **extricated** from his kennel.
   freed, released, saved
6. The massive army stood **formidably** just to their west.
   threateningly, imposingly, dangerously, intimidatingly
7. People always recognize **duplicity** in others before they recognize it in themselves.
   dishonesty, hypocrisy, falsehood, deceit
8. The brave fireman was finally able to **extricate** the victims from the room just before the roof collapsed.
   save, remove, extract, rescue

Mastery Substitution

Use a word from the Mastery Word List to replace the highlighted word or phrase.
You may have to change the form of the word to fit the sentence.

1. He greets everyone he meets with great **joy and excitement**. mirth
2. "Never yield to force; never yield to the apparently **overwhelming** might of the enemy." - Winston Churchill formidable
3. Rapunzel desperately wished for someone to **rescue** her from her tower prison. extricate
4. A severe **reluctance** overtook him when he was asked to move the delicate vase. qualm
5. The rope unexpectedly broke, **releasing** the horse from the burden of the plow. extricating
6. They discovered that the charge on the credit card was not due to the mistake of an innocent clerk, but to the cruel **deception** of a con man. duplicity
7. Lucy thought it was disgusting to put ketchup on macaroni and cheese, but Bobby had no such **revulsions**. qualms
8. It became obvious that the witness's account was **fallacious** when he mentioned being at two different places at the same time. duplicitous

Implementation

Use at least five of the words from the Mastery Word List in a paragraph of your own.

Vocabulary

Write the meaning of each bold word or phrase.

1. the little **gallipot** of a boat n. a small pot used by doctors as a container for ointments
2. The **gunwale** was lipping astern. n. the upper edge of the side of a vessel
3. He looked to the **priming** of his gun. n. the readying; the preparing
4. The ebb-tide … was now making **reparation**, and delaying our **assailants** n. amends; compensation; repair … n. assaulters; attackers
5. The other three took complete **headers**, and came up again n. headlong dives or falls
6. he had carried his over his shoulder by a **bandoleer** n. a broad cartridge belt worn over the shoulder by soldiers
7. he had not uttered one word of surprise, complaint, fear, or even **acquiescence*** n. yielding; acceptance; submission
8. We had no **ricochet** to fear. n. bounce; rebound
9. Silver was in the **stern-sheets** in command. n. the stern area of an open boat

*Look up "acquiesce" in the dictionary, and write out the complete definition, the alternate forms, and 2-3 synonyms. v. to accept or consent silently; to raise no opposition

alternate forms: acquienscence - n. acquienscent - adj.

synonyms: accomodate, accept, yield, agree, comply, consent, agree with reluctance

Comprehension Questions

Answer the following in complete sentences.

1. How does the captain's well-planned course of action suddenly go awry? The captain and his men had forgotten about the weapon still left to the mutineers: a cannon. Israel Hands, who was Flint's gunner, is now at the cannon, preparing to fire on them. Although no one gets hurt, the captain's boat sinks and they end up losing half their powder and provisions.
2. Why is the doctor concerned about Hunter and Joyce standing firm at the stockade? He is concerned because they are sure to be outnumbered. And although Hunter is certainly steady, Joyce is "not entirely fitted for a man of war."

3. What happens to Redruth? How does the squire react? *After they kill one of the mutineers, the mutineers strike back, shooting Redruth, who then dies. The squire kneels beside Redruth, kisses his hand, and cries like a child, asking for Redruth's forgiveness.

4. What does the captain insist on doing? And how does this "foolishness" prove to be a wise course of action? *The captain insists on hanging the British flag outside the stockade. Although alerting the mutineers to their location, they feel it is "a piece of stout, seamanly, good feeling" and shows their enemies that they despise their cannonade. They also know where to expect the cannonballs to be fired, so they are not caught off guard. The flag also alerts Jim to their presence.

5. What do the men find when they go out to retrieve the provisions that fell into the water when their jolly-boat sank? They find the mutineers have carried off their provisions and now, somehow, each of Silver's men are armed with a musket.

Quotations

Identify the speaker of the following.

"Carpet bowls! My lady's maid couldn't miss." Captain Smollett

"Be I going, doctor?" Redruth

"It mayn't be good divinity, but it's a fact." Smollett (to the squire)

"Strike my colors! No, sir, not I." Smollett

Discussion Questions

1. The squire was useless on the ship, but then proves to be a deadly shot. What causes the sudden change in the squire?
2. Redruth is described as laying "like a Trojan" behind his mattress. What is meant by this reference?

Enrichment

1. Research what a *long nine* is. Draw a detailed picture.
2. Make your own flag to hang in your room.

Reading Notes

Jolly Roger the black flag of pirates; usually depicted with a skull and crossbones

Union Jack the national flag of the United Kingdom

Vocabulary

Write the meaning of each bold word or phrase.

1. Reasons of his own; that's the **mainstay**. n. anchor, chief support
2. the wood still **flourished*** high and dense v. grew vigorously, thrived
3. towards the sea with a large **admixture** of live-oaks. n. a minor thing added to a mixture
4. I was put **sentry** at the door. n. guard, lookout
5. And you never saw me take **snuff**. n. smokeless tobacco inhaled through the nose
6. each had a good **stiff** glass of brandy adj. potent, strong

*Look up "flourish" in the dictionary, and write out the complete definition, the alternate forms, and 2-3 synonyms. v. & n. v. 1. to thrive or grow well 2. to prosper; to be successful 3. to be in a period of greatest influence; to be in one's prime 4. to make bold, ostentacious movements n. 1. a dramatic gesture 2. an ornamental or verbal embellishment

alternate forms: flourishes - n. flourishing - adj.

synonyms: v. prosper, grow, mature, develop, thrive, succeed; n. gesture, wave, embellishment

Comprehension Questions

Answer the following in complete sentences.

1. Why doesn't Ben Gunn go with Jim into the stockade? What are the "reasons of his own"?
Ben wants to make a proposal to the doctor or the squire before he joins them. He is also afraid Silver might be around. The "reasons of his own" are to be the conditions of his proposal that must be met before joining them.

2. What does Captain Smollett do to keep everyone from being depressed? The captain keeps them busy. He divides the group into watches, then sends men out to gather firewood and some to dig a grave for Redruth. The doctor is named cook, and Jim stands watch at the door. The captain also goes around to each man, to keep up his spirits and help out if needed.

3. What does the doctor tell Jim he will give to Ben Gunn? Why? The doctor says he will give Ben Gunn the piece of Parmesan cheese he keeps in his snuff-box. The doctor wants to give Ben this cheese because he knows he has a fancy for it, and it would be good to have another man on their side.

4. What is the group's "best hope" for survival? *Their best hope to avoid starvation is to kill off as many of the mutineers as possible so they will retreat. Any time there is a chance to kill them, they are to take it.

5. What are the group's "two able allies"? Explain. The group's two allies are rum and the climate. The mutineers are drunk on wine, which keeps them clumsy and off their guard. The location of the mutineers' camp and their lack of medicine has the doctor convinced they'll be sick within a week.

Quotations

Identify the speaker of the following.

"You're a good boy, or I'm mistook; but you're only a boy, all told." Ben Gunn (to Jim)

"That man Smollett is a better man than I am. And when I say that it means a deal, Jim." Dr. Livesey

"A man who has been three years biting his nails on a desert island, Jim, can't expect to appear as sane as you or me." Dr. Livesey (about Ben Gunn)

"First ship that ever I lost." Captain Smollett (about the Hispaniola)

Discussion Questions

1. What is the Jolly Roger? What is the Union Jack? What is their significance?
2. What does it mean that the doctor "staked his wig"?

Enrichment

1. Draw a picture of the Jolly Roger and the Union Jack.
2. Write a short essay on how the general opinion of Captain Smollett has changed since the beginning of the voyage. Include specific examples.

Vocabulary

Write the meaning of each bold word or phrase.

1. Silver himself, standing **placidly** by. adv. in a quiet and peaceful manner
2. crawled during the night out of the **morass**. n. bog or marsh
3. seeing how **cavalier** had been the captain's answer. adj. scornful, disdainful
4. He had been growing **nettled** before adj. annoyed, irritated
5. I'll give you my **affy-davy** upon my word of honor n. (slang for *affidavit*) a formal sworn statement of fact
6. Growling the foulest **imprecations** n. curses
7. the **resin** melting in the logs of the block-house. n. a sticky substance produced by certain trees and some other plants
8. "Thank you, sir," returned Joyce with the same quiet **civility**. n. politeness; consideration
9. with a loud **huzza**, a little cloud of pirates leaped from the woods n. cheer
10. as the blow still hung **impending** adj. looming, approaching, threatening
11. When I had first **sallied** from the door v. rushed
12. at any moment the fire might **recommence**. v. start again

Comprehension Questions

Answer the following in complete sentences.

1. What caused Silver to come seeking a truce? What does Jim have an "inkling" about?
Someone came into the mutineers' camp the previous night and attacked them, killing one of their men, which caused Silver to seek a truce. Jim has an inkling that it was Ben Gunn who attacked, although the captain remains confused by it.
2. What are the terms of Silver's truce? Silver says if they give him the map with the treasure's location on it, and stop killing his men, he'll let them live. He offers them a ride back on the ship to a safe location, or to give them enough provisions to remain behind on the island until he sends another ship to retrieve them.
3. What is the captain's response to Silver's terms? The captain refuses to give up the treasure map, but he's willing to take Silver and his men back to England in handcuffs for a fair trial. Smollett claims the mutineers can't find the treasure, can't sail the ship, and can't fight them. He also states that the next time he sees Silver, he'll put a bullet in his back.

4. Describe the reversal of positions Jim mentions. At first the captain's men have the advantage, being concealed in the fort, attacking Silver's exposed men. Then Silver's men reach the fort, and the captain's men are exposed and unable to return the attack.

5. Who wins the battle, and what is the price they had to pay for their victory? By how many men are they now outnumbered? *The captain's men have won the battle, but Joyce is dead, and Hunter and the captain are wounded. Now they are outnumbered eight to four. (They think nine to four.)

Quotations

Identify the speaker of the following.

"Cap'n, is it? My heart, and here's promotion!" Smollett (to himself about Silver)

"And what's more I would see you and him and this whole island blown clean out of the water into blazes first." Smollett (to Silver)

"Laugh, by thunder, laugh! Before an hour's out, ye'll laugh upon the other side. Them that die'll be the lucky ones." Silver (to Smollett and his men)

"I thought you had worn the king's coat!" Smollett (to the doctor)

"At 'em, all hands—all hands!" Job Anderson

"Round the house, lads! round the house!" Smollett

Discussion Questions

1. Who do you think is more confident of his group at the end of Chapter 20—Captain Smollett or Silver? Explain.
2. What do you think will be the final outcome of the battle? Why?

Enrichment

1. Write a paragraph explaining what Captain Smollett means when he says, "I'll see you all to Davy Jones."

"Davy Jones' Locker" is an expression used to mean the bottom of the sea: the resting place of drowned sailors. It means death at sea (to be sent to Davy Jones' Locker), whereas the name Davy Jones is a nickname for what would be the devil/saint/god of the seas.

Vocabulary

Write the meaning of each bold word or phrase.

1. I took the first step towards my **escapade** n. adventure; dangerous or risky undertaking
2. I was to go … **ascertain** whether it was there or not v. to determine; to find out
3. a certain tossing of **foliage** and grinding of boughs n. plant leaves
4. Ben Gunn's boat … was like the first and the worst **coracle** ever made by man. n. a small rounded boat made of waterproof material stretched over a wooden frame
5. you would have thought I had had enough of **truantry** for once. n. *truancy:* absence; shirking; absence without leave
6. I had taken another **notion** n. idea; whim; impulse
7. the mutineers, after their **repulse** of the morning n. a defeat; a check
8. the defeated pirates lay **carousing** in the swamp. v. engaging in boisterous, drunken merrymaking

Comprehension Questions

Answer the following in complete sentences.

1. Where does Jim believe the doctor is heading? *Jim believes the doctor is heading to see Ben Gunn.
2. What is it that overcomes Jim almost as strong as fear? What does this cause him to feel and do? His disgust with the stockade overwhelms him. He is hot and sweaty and surrounded by blood and dead bodies. This makes him envious of the doctor walking in the cool shade, with the sound of birds singing and the smell of the trees. This disgust and envy causes him to set off on his own expedition to find Ben Gunn's boat.

3. As Jim gets closer to the mutineers, what sound does he hear? What is the source of this sound? He hears "the most horrid, unearthly screaming." He soon realizes it is coming from Captain Flint, Silver's parrot.

4. What is Jim's plan? *Jim's plan is to cut the Hispaniola adrift, so the mutineers can't take her out to sea.

5. What are the "two points" visible to Jim on the whole anchorage? The first point is the great fire on the shore where the mutineers lay. The other point indicates the position of the anchored ship.

Quotations

Identify the speaker of the following.

"Well, shipmate, mad he may not be; but if he's not, you mark my words, I am!" Gray (to Jim, about the doctor)

Discussion Questions

1. Jim called leaving the stockade his "second folly," far worse than his first; and yet at the same time he mentioned it would help in saving them. Explain this paradox. Have you ever experienced making a big mistake that turned out to be "providential"?
2. Do you think Jim has a good plan? Do you think it will succeed? Why or why not? If in his position, what would you do?

Enrichment

1. Draw a picture of Ben Gunn's boat, as described in the book.
2. Find the definitions of the following nautical terms in the index: *bulwarks*, *thwart.*

Vocabulary

Write the meaning of each bold word or phrase.

1. turning round and round was the **manoeuvre** she was best at. n. strategic or tactical military or naval movement (modern spelling: maneuver)
2. a ditty rather too **dolefully** appropriate adv. sorrowfully
3. all these buccaneers were as **callous*** as the sea they sailed on. adj. heartless; indifferent
4. just as I gave the last **impulsion**, my hands came across a light cord n. a thrust; a push
5. little ripples, coming over with a sharp, bristling sound and slightly **phosphorescent**. adj. characterized by or emitting light
6. until sleep at last **supervened** v. followed closely; ensued
7. loud **reverberations** … succeeded one another from second to second n. echoes; sound reflections
8. spending my strength in vain to scale the **beetling crags**. adj. jutting or overhanging … n. rocks or bluffs
9. there was no **contrariety** between [the wind] and the current n. the quality or condition of being contrary (opposed)
10. I saw I must **infallibly*** miss that point adv. certainly; incapable of erring
11. I felt sure I should make the next **promontory** without fail. n. a natural elevation (especially a rocky one that juts out into the sea)

*Look up the following words in the dictionary, and write out the complete definition, the alternate forms, and 2-3 synonyms for each word.

callous: adj. emotionally hardened; unfeeling and indifferent to the suffering/feelings of others
alternate forms: callously - adv. callousness - n. *synonyms:* heartless, insensitive, cold, apathetic, impassive (Note: A *callus* is a rough piece of skin.)

infallible: adj. without fault or weakness; incapable of error
alternate forms: infallibility - n. infallibly - adv.
synonyms: unerring, dependable, absolute, reliable, unfailing

Comprehension Questions

Answer the following in complete sentences.

1. What does Jim remember prior to cutting the rope that attaches the ship to the anchor? How does this change his course of action? Jim remembers that if a rope is cut while it is taut, it is very dangerous, and could possibly knock him and his boat out of the water. He decides to wait until the tide shifts the ship and slackens the rope before cutting.

2. How and why does Jim decide to take a look through one of the cabin windows? What does he see? When Jim instinctively grabs a swinging cord from the ship, his curiosity gets the better of him. He sees Israel Hands and another man wrestling with each other, their hands upon each other's throats.

3. How does Jim react to his impending doom at the end of Chapter 23? **Jim resigns himself to being caught by the men on board the ship. He lays down in the coracle and "devoutly recommended [his] spirit to its Maker." He expects to drift into breaking waters, which will kill him quickly. Although he admits to being able to bear dying, he cannot bear to watch his death approaching.

4. Explain Jim's strategy to maneuver the coracle. Jim has to lie down in the boat to not disturb its balance, so it can thread its way through the waves. In smooth places, Jim can put the paddle over the side and give a shove or two in the direction he wants to go. This is exhaustingly slow work, but effective.

5. What does Jim think when he sees the Hispaniola at sea? What does this lead him to plan? He realizes the ship is not being steered, so he thinks the men are either drunk or have deserted the ship. He decides to get on board and "return the vessel to her captain."

Quotations

Identify the speaker of the following.

"But one man of her crew alive what put to sea with seventy-five." one of the mutineers

"Clumsy fellows, they must still be drunk as owls." Jim (about the men on board the Hispaniola)

Discussion Questions

1. Did you know what Jim was planning when he went in search of Ben Gunn's coracle? Was his mission a success? Why or why not?

Enrichment

1. Find the definitions of the following nautical terms: *hawser* (in index), *yaw*, *skiff*, *billows*, *tiller* (in index), *tack* (in index), *forefoot* (in index), *jib-boom* (in index), *stay*, *swell.*

   yaw: swerve … *skiff*: small boat … *billows*: large waves … *stay*: heavy rope or cable … *swell*: crestless wave

Mastery Word List

acquiesce **callous** **flourish** **infallible**

Synonym Substitution

Write a few good synonyms or a phrase in the blank to replace the highlighted word.

1. Mushrooms **flourish** in dark, damp areas. thrive, grow, develop, multiply
2. "An **infallible** method of making fanatics is to persuade before you instruct." - Voltaire
   unfailing, effective, conclusive, undeniable
3. The **callous** man simply continued walking after bumping into the child and knocking her down.
   unfeeling, cruel, emotionally hardened
4. Her failure to **acquiesce** to the wishes of her mother resulted in not being able to go to the party.
   comply, accept, submit, consent
5. With a **flourish** and a bow she bid farewell to her audience.
   wild gesture, grand movement

Mastery Substitution

Use a word from the Mastery Word List to replace the highlighted word or phrase.
You may have to change the form of the word to fit the sentence.

1. The willingness to **comply** to authority is an important skill to learn during your youth.
   acquiesce
2. Being unwilling to be moved by the misfortune of others is not an act of toughness but **emotional hardness.** callousness
3. Even though he struggled with math last year, this year he is **progressing well**.
   flourishing
4. Though I do not doubt your honesty, I do, however, doubt your **correctness**.
   infallibility
5. After adding many **unnecessary decorations** to his car, he proceeded to cruise the avenue.
   flourishes
6. No one would **accept** such harsh peace terms. acquiesce to
7. His sister **cruelly** threw his favorite toy in the trash. callously
8. When he suggested that humans could fly if they swallowed enough helium, Mark started to believe that Brian wasn't **always right** after all. infallible

Implementation

Use all four words from the Mastery Word List in a paragraph of your own.

Reading Notes

O'Brien the seaman with the red cap; killed by Israel Hands

Vocabulary

Write the meaning of each bold word or phrase.

1. the ship kept bucking and **sidling** like a vicious horse v. moving sideways
2. the whole body **canting** towards the stern v. slanting
3. the lamp still cast a smoky glow, **obscure** and brown as **umber**. adj. unclear; indistinct … n. a natural brown earth pigment
4. **Foraging** about, I found a bottle with some brandy left v. searching for food or provisions
5. Why, I ain't such an **infernal** lubber, after all. adj. extremely evil or cruel; fiendish
6. I was greatly **elated** with my new command adj. excited, delighted, proud
7. my conscience, which had **smitten** me hard for my desertion v. afflicted; struck with a heavy blow
8. a **haggard** old man's smile; but there was, besides that, a grain of **derision** adj. appearing worn and exhausted; gaunt … n. mockery; ridicule

Comprehension Questions

Answer the following in complete sentences.

1. Describe the state of the Hispaniola as Jim finds it. Jim finds the Hispaniola with no one steering it. The whole ship shudders and groans as it is tossed about on the sea. He sees the man in the red cap and Israel Hands slumped over, as though dead, with blood surrounding them. The cabin below is a mess, with mud and empty bottles everywhere, and one of the doctor's books torn apart. All of the barrels of wine are gone.
2. What are the emotions going through Jim at the state of Israel Hands? When Jim hears Israel Hands moaning in pain, he instinctively feels pity for him, but when he remembers what he heard while in the apple barrel, all pity leaves him. He does bring him brandy for the pain, but not before he takes his own long drink of water. He never forgets that Israel Hands is a mutineer and not to be trusted.

3. What bargain does Jim strike with Israel Hands? *The coxswain requests food, drink, and a scarf to bandage his leg in exchange for showing Jim how to sail the ship to North Inlet.

4. How does Jim feel about his new position? He feels "elated" about taking command of the Hispaniola. He is pleased with the good weather and with having plenty of water and food. He had felt bad about leaving his group at the stockade, but now his "great conquest" has eased his conscience.

5. Explain the foreboding in the last sentence of this chapter. While Jim is busy about the ship, the coxswain watches him continually with a look of derision on his face, as though he knows something that Jim does not. The author's vocabulary enhances the foreboding: the smile appeared "continually"; "derision"; "treachery"; "craftily"; and the repetition of "watched, and watched, and watched."

Quotations

Identify the speaker of the following.

"Brandy." Israel Hands

"I don't have no manner of luck, you see, and that's what's the matter with me."
Israel Hands

"I've come aboard to take possession of this ship, Mr. Hands; and you'll please regard me as your captain until further notice." Jim

"God save the King! and there's an end to Captain Silver!"
Jim (after taking down the Jolly Roger and throwing it into the sea)

Discussion Questions

1. Why do you think Jim waits to give the brandy to Israel until after he's had a good, deep drink of water himself?
2. Why does Jim say, "Better none than these" when taking down the Jolly Roger?
3. What is your impression of Israel Hands? Do you think Jim made a good bargain with him?

Vocabulary

Write the meaning of each bold word or phrase.

1. The whole story was a **pretext**. n. fictitious reason; excuse

2. I think I was a good, prompt **subaltern** n. a subordinate; a person of inferior rank or position

3. the space was longer and narrower, and more like … the **estuary** of a river n. the wide mouth of a river; inlet

4. we saw the wreck of a ship in the last stages of **dilapidation***. n. a state of disrepair

5. had not a sudden **disquietude** seized upon me n. a state of uneasiness; anxiety

6. his face itself as red as a red **ensign** with his haste and fury. n. a flag or banner

7. a moment or two passed in **feints** on his part n. fake attacks to fool an enemy

8. We were both of us **capsized** in a second v. overturned; tipped over

9. I scarce can say it was by my own **volition*** n. a conscious choice or decision; will

*Look up the following words in the dictionary, and write out the complete definition, the alternate forms, and 2-3 synonyms for each word.

dilapidate: v. to fall or cause to fall into ruin or disuse

alternate forms: dilapidated - adj. dilapidation - n.

synonyms: v. ruin, destroy, wreck; adj. neglected, falling apart, decrepit, old, rickety

volition: n. 1. a conscious decision or choice 2. the mental power or ability of choice; the will

alternate forms: volitional - adj. volitionally - adv. volitive - adj.

synonyms: free will, choice, discretion, desire

Comprehension Questions

Answer the following in complete sentences.

1. Describe how Jim finds out that Israel Hands is planning on killing him. *Jim can tell that the coxswain is lying when he asks for some wine, so while he goes below deck to fetch some wine, he sneaks back up to watch what Hands does. Jim sees him hide a knife in his jacket and go back to the position he was in when Jim left.

2. When Israel Hands complains about dying, what does Jim advise him to do? What is Hands' response to this, and how does Jim react? Jim advises Hands to pray "like a Christian man." Hands asks him why, and Jim heatedly responds by pointing out that Hands has lived in "sin and lies and blood" and that a man he killed lies at his feet. "For God's mercy, Mr. Hands, that's why." Jim is so upset because he knows that Hands plans to kill him as well.

3. Why does Jim feel confident about his stance against Hands, even after his guns initially do not work? When they are one-on-one, dodging each other, Jim feels confident because he has played this "boy's game" many times before, and because Hands is an "elderly seaman with a wounded thigh."

4. What weakness in Jim almost becomes his downfall? Explain. *Jim's cockiness almost becomes his downfall, because as he finds himself in an advantageous position, pointing two loaded pistols at Hands, he lets down his guard, and doesn't expect Hands to throw his knife at him.

5. What is the outcome of the battle? When Hands throws his knife at Jim, pinning his shoulder to the mast, Jim's guns go off, shooting Hands, who falls into the water.

Quotations

Identify the speaker of the following.

"You can kill the body, Mr. Hands, but not the spirit; you must know that already." Jim

"I'm for my long home, and no mistake." Israel Hands

"Jim, I reckon we're fouled, you and me, and we'll have to sign articles." Israel Hands

Discussion Questions

1. How does Jim know that the coxswain is lying when he says he prefers wine to brandy?
2. Why do you think the author ended the chapter the way he did?

Enrichment

1. What is Israel Hands' philosophy of life? Write a few sentences explaining it.

   Hands says that he hasn't seen good come of goodness, so he prefers to be the one that strikes first, because "dead men don't bite." Basically he looks out for his own good in all situations, no matter what that may result in him doing.

Vocabulary

Write the meaning of each bold word or phrase.

1. I **desisted** with a violent shudder. v. stopped; ceased
2. nor did it greatly **gall** me when I used my arm. v. irritate; aggravate
3. he lay like some horrible, **ungainly** sort of puppet adj. clumsy; awkward
4. the strain was so heavy that I half feared to **meddle**. v. to interfere; to tamper
5. I walked more **circumspectly**, keeping an eye on every side. adv. prudently, heedful of circumstances and potential consequences
6. I slacked my pace and went a **trifle warily**. n. a small amount … adv. watchfully, on guard
7. they kept an **infamous** bad watch adv. (infamously) notoriously; disgracefully

Comprehension Questions

Answer the following in complete sentences.

1. What is Jim afraid of, more than the pain in his shoulder? Rather than fearing his wound, he fears falling from the mast into the water where Israel Hands lies.
2. Describe Jim's emotions as he sets out to find his friends. Jim desires nothing more than to find his friends at the stockade and boast of his achievements. Although they might blame him for deserting them, he feels confident that once they realize he's recaptured the ship, they will believe his time away was well spent. He is in "famous spirits."
3. What does he see on his way? What does he assume it is? Jim sees a glow in the sky, and he assumes it is Ben Gunn roasting his dinner over a fire. He wonders how Ben Gunn could be so careless to show his presence, for if Jim sees the fire, Silver and his men could also see it.

4. What causes wonder and terror in Jim as he nears the camp? What puts him back at ease?
As Jim nears his camp, he sees a large fire smoldering. Because he knows that Captain Smollett always ordered them to use firewood sparingly, he wonders if something has gone wrong. *He soon forgets his fear as he hears what he believes is the snoring of his friends.

5. Describe what happens once Jim is inside the camp. Jim's foot strikes a sleeper's leg, causing Silver's parrot to begin squawking, "Pieces of eight!" alerting the men to Jim's presence. Jim tries to escape, but just runs into the arms of his captors.

Quotations

Identify the speaker of the following.

"Pieces of eight! pieces of eight! pieces of eight! pieces of eight!" Silver's parrot

"Who goes?" Silver

Discussion Questions

1. Which apprehensions should Jim have heeded when heading back to camp?
2. Where do you think Jim's friends are?

Enrichment

1. Create your own scenario where Jim escapes capture.
2. Write a one-page description of your scenario and share with the class.

Vocabulary

Write the meaning of each bold word or phrase.

1. The parrot sat, **preening** her plumage v. smoothing or cleaning (feathers) with beak or bill
2. stick the **glim** in the wood heap n. a source of light, as a candle
3. I stood there, looking Silver in the face, **pluckily** enough adv. in a manner having or showing courage and spirit in trying circumstances
4. the cabin party were **incensed*** at me for my desertion v. made angry, enraged
5. cried Silver **truculently** adv. in a hostile or destructive manner; fiercely
6. his eye kept wandering **furtively** adv. stealthily; shiftily; expressing hidden motives
7. I know a lad that's **staunch**. adj. trustworthy, loyal

*Look up "incense" in the dictionary, and write out the complete definition, the alternate forms, and 2-3 synonyms.

v. to anger or enrage

alternate forms: incensed - adj.

synonyms: disgust, madden, exasperate, provoke, infuriate

Comprehension Questions

Answer the following in complete sentences.

1. What does Silver tell Jim about his friends? How does Jim feel about this information?
   Silver tells Jim he struck a bargain with the doctor. Silver let them go free in exchange for the block-house, firewood, brandy, and their food. He claims the doctor said he and his men were sick of Jim and didn't care where he was. Jim is happy his friends are still alive, and he partly believes what Silver says. He is more relieved than distressed by this news.
2. How does Jim respond when Silver asks him to choose to join his men or be on his own, and what does he offer? *Jim admits to hearing Silver's plan in the apple barrel and to everything he'd accomplished since then. Jim says if Silver spares his life, he'll defend them in court. "Kill another and do yourselves no good, or spare me and keep a witness to save you from the gallows."
3. How do the men respond to Silver when he comes to Jim's defense after Morgan wants to kill him?
   The men are dissatisfied. They whisper together while looking at Silver, then decide to hold a council outside the house to discuss the situation amongst themselves, and one by one they leave with a salute and an apology.

4. Describe Silver's plan involving Jim. What does Jim begin to understand? Silver believes his men are going to mutiny against him, so he says he will stay by Jim's side through thick and thin. He'll save Jim's life if Jim defends him in court, keeping him from being hanged. Jim begins to understand that "all is lost."

5. What does Silver reveal to Jim at the end of the chapter? *Silver asks Jim why the doctor gave him the treasure map, which Jim knew nothing about.

Quotations

Identify the speaker of the following.

"The laugh's on my side; I've had the top of this business from the first." Jim

"Cross me, and you'll go where many a good man's gone before you …" Silver (to Morgan)

"But, you mark, I stand by you through thick and thin." Silver (to Jim)

"What I can do, that I'll do." Jim (to Silver)

Discussion Questions

1. Describe Jim's relationship with Silver.
2. Do you think Jim made a good decision regarding his deal with Silver? Why or why not?

Enrichment

1. Research what Silver means by telling his men, "Perhaps you can understand King George's English."
2. Find the meanings of the following terms used in the narrative's context: *rum puncheon*, *marlin-spike*, *caulker.*

1. King George supposedly was unable to speak English (which led to unpopularity among the people), however this inability may not have existed later in his reign, as documents from that time show that he understood, spoke, and wrote English.

2. *rum puncheon*: a high proof rum; so a "son of a rum puncheon" most likely means a son of a drunk.

marlinspike: a pointed iron hand tool that is used to separate strands of a rope or cable. In the text, the seaman is saying that the crew doesn't like bullying one bit, as in a single strand.

caulk: to pack the seams between the planks of the bottom of a vessel with waterproof material to prevent leakage. In the text, Silver is saying a drink will keep him steady (avoid sinking like a leaking ship).

Reading Notes

George Merry buccaneer with yellow eyes; accuses Silver of ruining the trip

Vocabulary

Write the meaning of each bold word or phrase.

1. this **emissary** retired again n. a person sent on a special mission
2. I won't hurt a **deputation**. n. a person or group appointed to represent others; a delegate
3. you don't be under no kind of **apprehension** n. fearful or uneasy anticipation of the future; dread
4. he had been talking with a **vehemence** that shook the house. n. a display of strong feeling; fierceness
5. you, George Merry, that had the **ague shakes** upon you not six hours agone n. chills and fever
6. the dark perils that **environed** v. surrounded; bordered

Comprehension Questions

Answer the following in complete sentences.

1. What do the buccaneers return with for Silver? *The buccaneers hand over the black spot to Silver, made on a page torn from Dick's Bible. It reads, "Depposed." They are basically overthrowing him as their captain.
2. What are George's four grievances against Silver? George says Silver 1) made a mess (hash) of the cruise, 2) let the enemy go for nothing, 3) wouldn't let the men attack the enemy when retreating, and 4) saved Jim's life.
3. What is Silver's response to these grievances? Silver responds that 1) Anderson and Hands made a mess of the cruise, not him, 2) everyone agreed on the bargain with the enemy because they were starving for food, 3) they need a doctor on hand, and 4) Jim is their hostage when an enemy consort comes by.

4. What does Silver reveal? How do the buccaneers respond? Silver pulls out the treasure map for all the men to see. The buccaneers immediately respond by reinstating him as their leader. While touching the map, they act as though they are already touching the gold while safely at sea on the ship.

5. What does Jim think about as he falls asleep? Jim thinks about the man he killed that day, as well as the danger he had been in. He also thinks of Silver's current predicament: "keeping the mutineers together with one hand, and grasping, with the other … to make his peace and save his miserable life." *Jim feels bad for Silver, wicked as he is, because of all the dangers surrounding him and the death by hanging that surely awaits him.

Quotations

Identify the speaker of the following.

"The black spot! I thought so." Silver

"You're a funny man, by your account; but you're over now …" George (to Silver)

"We'll all swing and sun-dry for your bungling." George (to Silver)

"Barbecue for ever! Barbecue for cap'n!" the buccaneers (after Silver reveals the map)

Discussion Questions

1. What was Silver trying to do by pointing out the fact that the men had used a page from the Bible to deliver the black spot?
2. Has your opinion of Silver changed at all?

Enrichment

1. Silver again refers to "Execution Dock by London town." If you did not research this reference from Chapter 11, do so now. Share your findings with the class.

Mastery Word List

dilapidate **volition** **incense**

Synonym Substitution

Write a few good synonyms or a phrase in the blank to replace the highlighted word.

1. Sally went to the library to do her homework of her own **volition**. conscious choice, decision, will
2. The unoccupied house was beginning to **dilapidate**.
   ruin, destroy, wreck
3. The rude comment was meant to **incense** the opposing team.
   madden, exasperate, provoke, infuriate
4. He exercised his **volition** when he voted against the politician.
   free will, choice, discretion

Mastery Substitution

Use a word from the Mastery Word List to replace the highlighted word or phrase.
You may have to change the form of the word to fit the sentence.

1. The family would have to repair the roof on the **neglected** house before moving in.
   dilapidated
2. The dog acted of its own **conscious choice**, snatching the meat off the table and ensuring its punishment. volition
3. The actors were **angered** by the teenagers who talked during the entire play.
   incensed
4. The **decrepit state** of the painting drastically reduced the value.
   dilapidation
5. The child tried to **provoke** the babysitter by throwing food at her.
   incense
6. The speech was a **willing** act on the part of the witness. volitional

Implementation

Use all three words from the Mastery Word List in a paragraph of your own.

Vocabulary

Write the meaning of each bold word or phrase.

1. I remembered with confusion my **insubordinate** and stealthy conduct. adj. not submissive to authority; disobedient or rebellious
2. not having enough sense to know … the dry land from a vile**, pestiferous slough**. adj. dirty, harmful … n. a swamp or miry place
3. you don't appear to me to have the **rudiments*** of a notion n. the elementary stages of any subject; "ABCs"
4. his last night's victory had given him a huge **preponderance** on their minds. n. superiority in weight, force, importance, or influence
5. till then I'll **gammon** that doctor, if I have to ile his boots with brandy. v. to mislead by deceptive talk
6. silenced by his **volubility** rather than convinced. n. constant talking, fluency

*Look up the following words in the dictionary, and write out the complete definition, the alternate forms, and 2-3 synonyms for each word.

rudiment/rudimentary: *rudiment:* n. 1. a fundamental aspect of a subject 2. something in an undeveloped form *rudimentary:* adj. 1. involving basic principles 2. undeveloped

alternate forms: rudimentarily - adv.

synonyms.: n. basics, essentials; adj. elementary, basic, simple, unrefined, rough

Comprehension Questions

Answer the following in complete sentences.

1. When the doctor comes to the mutineers' camp, how does he treat them? How do the mutineers respond to their guest? The doctor treats the mutineers for their wounds and ailments as though nothing has happened, and they respond to him as though nothing has happened: "… as if he were still ship's doctor, and they still faithful hands before the mast." Although the doctor is friendly, he also refers to himself as a prison doctor and says he is keeping them alive for King George to hang them. He says Silver is at fault for their ailments because they've camped in a bog. The mutineers take his medicine with "laughable humility, more like charity school-children than blood-guilty mutineers and pirates."

2. Of what do the mutineers accuse Silver? Are they right or wrong? When Silver allows the doctor to speak to Jim alone, the mutineers accuse him of "playing double," trying to make peace for himself with the doctor while sacrificing the interests of his comrades. Yes, they are right about this; this is exactly what Silver is doing.

3. How does Silver gain back his crew's loyalty? Silver calls them fools, waves the treasure map in their faces, and points out it would be a bad idea to break the treaty when they're about to go treasure hunting. He claims he will be swindling the doctor over until it is time for them to break the treaty. Although the crew is still not entirely convinced, they stop accusing him of disloyalty.

4. Why is Jim not afraid of death? What is it that Jim *is* afraid of? Jim is not afraid of death, for he feels he deserves it, but he is afraid of being tortured for information. He tells the doctor if he is tortured, he will give up the location of the ship.

5. What deal does the doctor strike with Silver? The doctor agrees to come to Silver's defense in court if they both get out alive. He advises Silver to keep Jim close by his side and call for help when needed.

Quotations

Identify the speaker of the following.

"Block-house, ahoy! Here's the doctor." Dr. Livesey

"I make it a point of honour not to lose a man for King George (God bless him!) and the gallows." Dr. Livesey

"Doctor, I'm no coward! no, not I—not so much!" Silver

"There is a kind of fate in this." Dr. Livesey (to Jim)

Discussion Questions

1. Why does the doctor tell Jim, "There is a kind of fate in this"? Do you agree?
2. Do you admire Jim for keeping his word to Silver? What would you have done?

Enrichment

1. Of what do the words *forfeit*, *perjury*, and *concession* remind you? Is there significance behind the author using these terms?
   These terms are used in a court of law: *forfeit*: to surrender or give up the right to, on account of an offense or a breach of contract; *perjury*: the deliberate, willful giving of false or incomplete testimony under oath; *concession*: the act of yielding or conceding, as to a demand or argument.

Reading Notes

Flint's Pointer/Allardyce the skeleton of one of Flint's crew; points the way to the treasure

Vocabulary

Write the meaning of each bold word or phrase.

1. Should the scheme he had now sketched prove **feasible** adj. capable of being accomplished or brought about; possible
2. their inexplicable **cession** of the chart n. the surrendering or relinquishing
3. The other men were variously **burthened**; some carrying picks and shovels adj. burdened; weighted down
4. his mutineers … must have been driven to **subsist** on clear water and the proceeds of their hunting. v. to exist, survive, live
5. it was not likely they would be very **flush** of powder. adj. marked by abundance; plentiful; overflowing
6. the terms of the note on the back … admitted of some **ambiguity**. n. vagueness, doubt, uncertainty
7. the rough cliffy **eminence** called the Mizzen-mast Hill. n. a rise of ground; a hill

Comprehension Questions

Answer the following in complete sentences.

1. Describe Jim's impression of the mutineers over breakfast, including Silver. Jim realizes how wasteful the men are, for they are cooking more than they need and burning the leftovers. He sees now that they are incapable of holding up their side of the battle for very long. He is surprised that Silver does not rebuke their recklessness.
2. How does Silver act over breakfast? Silver boasts about his clever ways to his men, saying he will find out where the ship is hidden, and once the ship is found, they will have the upper hand. Jim believes this boasting has restored Silver's men's hope and confidence in him, and has also restored Silver's hope and confidence in himself. He also says they will reward Jim for being their hostage once the treasure is found.

3. What are Jim's misgivings regarding Silver? regarding his friends? Jim knows that Silver has already proven himself a traitor, and may adopt his new plan with his own men if it proves possible, preferring wealth and freedom to "a bare escape from hanging." Even if Silver stays true to the doctor, when the mutineers realize this betrayal, Jim and Silver will be in danger for their life. On top of this, Jim is still confused about why his friends left the stockade and gave Silver the map, and by the doctor's warning to Silver.

4. What problem do the mutineers encounter as they use Flint's chart to hunt the treasure? The chart is ambiguous, so it is hard for them to tell exactly where to go. The chart indicates a tall tree as the principal mark, but there are many tall trees, and each of the men thinks a different one is the tall tree in question.

5. What do they discover? What is their reaction? *They discover the remains of one of Flint's men, Allardyce. It seems Flint has positioned the man's body to point in the direction of the treasure. The men are greatly shaken up by this discovery, and even worry about Flint's spirit being there. "The terror of the dead buccaneer had fallen on their spirits."

Quotations

Identify the speaker of the following.

"... we'll save our necks in spite of fate and fortune." Silver (to Jim)

"Look out for squalls when you find it." Dr. Livesey (to Silver - in previous chapter)

"Dear heart, but he died bad, did Flint!" mutineer with a bandage

"Care killed a cat. Fetch ahead for the doubloons." Silver (to his men)

Discussion Questions

1. What does living "hand to mouth" mean?
2. What do you think the doctor's warning to Silver, "Look out for squalls when you find it," means?

Enrichment

1. Make your own replica of Flint's chart, including the note on the back. Be as detailed as possible.
2. Research the type of food sailors had to eat. What is *junk*?

   Junk is hard salt beef for consumption on board a ship.

Vocabulary

Write the meaning of each bold word or phrase.

1. it's someone **skylarking**—someone that's flesh and blood v. romping or playing jokes
2. growing terror at the **irreverence** of his words. n. lack of reverence or due respect
3. It was **conspicuous** far to sea both to the east and west adj. clearly visible
4. Before us was a great **excavation** n. hole, mine, pit, ditch
5. All was clear to **probation**. n. a period of testing
6. The **cache** had been found and **rifled**. n. a place for concealment and safekeeping, as of valuables … v. ransacked or plundered; pillaged

Comprehension Questions

Answer the following in complete sentences.

1. "I never have seen men more dreadfully affected than the pirates. The colour went from their six faces like enchantment; some leaped to their feet, some clawed hold of others; Morgan grovelled on the ground." What is the cause of this commotion? Of what are the men convinced? Why? While hunting for the treasure, the men hear a voice singing the sailor's song. The pirates immediately assume the voice belongs to the spirit of Flint. Silver claims it must be a joke, but then they hear the voice say "Darby M'Graw" over and over, and then, "Fetch aft the rum, Darby!" The men are certain it is Flint's spirit, for those were the last words that Flint spoke before he died.
2. What does Silver say that upsets Merry? Then what does he say that calms the men down? Silver says nothing will stop him from seeking and finding the treasure, and that since he didn't fear Flint in life, he'll not fear him in death. "I'll not be beat by man nor devil." Merry gets very upset, advising Silver to not cross a spirit. Silver points out that the voice had an echo, and if spirits don't have a shadow, they shouldn't have echoes either. This fact, plus the conclusion that the voice must have been Ben Gunn's, revives their spirits.
3. Describe the change in the pirates when they near the treasure. As they near the treasure, the men completely forget their fear. "Their eyes burned in their heads; their feet grew speedier and lighter; their whole soul was bound up in that fortune …" Silver's nostrils quiver, he curses like a madman, and yanks on Jim's rope, while giving him "deadly" and "murderous" glares.

4. What does Jim think about Silver's changed attitude? What does he imagine Silver might do? Silver is like a man possessed, and it is evident to Jim that all his promises and the doctor's warning are forgotten. He imagines Silver hopes to seize the treasure, find and board the ship, cut every man's throat, and sail away with his treasure, as was his original intent.

5. What waits for the pirates where the treasure should be? The treasure is gone, but in its place is part of a pick and boards from packing-cases, bearing the name of Flint's ship, Walrus.

Quotations

Identify the speaker of the following.

"Fetch aft the rum, Darby!" the voice among the trees (Ben Gunn) (*Also Flint's last words)

"I'll not be beat by man nor devil." Silver

"Don't you cross a spirit." George Merry (to Silver, about Flint)

"Why, nobody minds Ben Gunn; dead or alive, nobody minds him." George Merry

Discussion Questions

1. Whose voice do you think was the voice among the trees? Why?
2. Why does Merry say that nobody minds Ben Gunn, dead or alive?
3. Did it surprise you that the nearness of treasure changed the mutineers' attitude?

Enrichment

1. Give your best impression of the ghostly voice.

Vocabulary

Write the meaning of each bold word or phrase.

1. I was so **revolted** at these constant changes adj. disgusted; nauseated
2. I could not **forbear** whispering v. to refrain from; to resist
3. "Dig away, boys," said Silver, with the coolest **insolence**. n. rudeness, disrespect
4. [they] were already **ambushed** before the arrival of the treasure-hunters. v. attacked by surprise from a concealed position
5. you're a **prodigious** villain and impostor adj. massive, tremendous
6. It is a gross **dereliction*** of my duty. n. a failure to carry out one's obligations, neglect
7. the same bland, polite, **obsequious** seaman of the voyage out. adj. servile, obedient, attentive

*Look up the following words in the dictionary, and write out the complete definition, the alternate forms, and 2-3 synonyms for each word.

derelict/dereliction: *derelict:* adj. 1. abandoned 2. negligent
n. 1. a forsaken person; an outcast 2. abandoned property (esp. a ship at sea)
dereliction: n. neglect of one's duty
adjective synonyms: unreliable, careless, delinquent, deserted, forsaken, disregarded

Comprehension Questions

Answer the following in complete sentences.

1. Describe Silver's final act as "double traitor." As soon as he realizes the treasure is gone, Silver decides his only hope is to side with Jim, so he immediately changes sides, giving Jim a pistol, and advising him to "stand by for trouble."
2. What is the reaction of the pirates to Silver's betrayal? They believe Silver knew the treasure wasn't there the whole time, and they plan to kill Silver and Jim, believing they have an advantage over a crippled man and a young boy.
3. Describe how Jim is saved. The doctor, Gray, and Ben Gunn appear just in time, shooting Merry and another pirate. The other three pirates turn and run away. The men make their way to the boats to escape to Ben Gunn's cave.

4. Who was the hero "from beginning to end"? Explain. Ben Gunn was the hero, for he had been the one to find the skeleton and the treasure. He dug up the treasure and carried it back to his cave. Once the doctor found this out, he gave the chart to Silver, as well as the provisions, for Ben Gunn had stocked his cave with plenty of food. Realizing Jim was with the mutineers, they decided to meet up at the treasure site ahead of the pirates. When they saw they were behind, Ben Gunn decided to play with their superstitions and call out to frighten them, which worked perfectly, allowing the doctor and Gray to arrive in time.

5. What is the reaction of Jim's friends to Silver? The doctor admits that if it weren't for Jim, he would have left Silver to be killed by the pirates. The squire calls Silver a villain and impostor. While the squire will not persecute him in trial, as promised, he still judges Silver for his crimes. The captain doesn't seem to be surprised at Silver's return, and doesn't say much to him.

Quotations

Identify the speaker of the following.

"So you've changed sides again." Jim (to Silver)

"One's the old cripple that brought us all here and blundered us down to this; the other's that cub that I mean to have the heart of." George Merry (to the other pirates)

"I reckon I settled you." Silver (to Merry, after shooting him)

"But the dead men, sir, hang about your neck like millstones." the squire (to Silver)

Discussion Questions

1. Who is the chieftain the chapter title refers to?
2. What does the squire mean when he says the dead men hang about Silver's neck like millstones?
3. Do you think anyone that hunted for the treasure deserved to find it? Explain.

Enrichment

1. Can you recall how many times Silver changed sides during the adventure? List his treacheries and their outcomes.
2. Draw a picture of Ben Gunn's cave as described in the book.
3. What is a *teetotum*? See if you can make one out of paper.
   teetotum: a spinning top, usually having four lettered sides, used to play various games of chance.

Vocabulary

Write the meaning of each bold word or phrase.

1. a strange collection, like Billy Bones's **hoard** for the diversity of coinage n. a hidden fund or supply stored for future use; a cache; stash
2. he kept on trying to **ingratiate** himself with all. v. to bring oneself into the favor or good graces of another, especially by deliberate effort
3. with their arms raised in **supplication**. n. a humble plea or entreaty
4. what with **baffling** winds and a couple of fresh gales v. impeding or hindering the force or movement of
5. he began, with wonderful **contortions**, to make a confession n. twistings; things in a twisted state
6. The maroon had **connived** at his escape in a shore boat v. cooperated secretly in an illegal or wrongful action; colluded; schemed; plotted
7. he still lives, a great favorite, though something of a **butt** n. one that serves as an object of ridicule or contempt

Comprehension Questions

Answer the following in complete sentences.

1. Describe the battling emotions towards Silver that Jim feels. Jim is tempted to be thankful to Silver for saving his life, but then again, he reasons, he has the most reason of anybody to think badly of him because he had seen Silver planning "a fresh treachery" when he'd thought he'd discovered the treasure.
2. Describe how the men leave the remaining pirates on the island. They leave the men with plenty of ammunition, salt goat, medicine, tools, clothing, a spare sail, rope, and some tobacco as a present. As they are leaving the island, they see the maroons on the beach begging not to be left behind. The men cannot risk another mutiny, so refuse to go back for them. One of the maroons takes a shot at the ship, which just barely misses Silver.

3. What happened to Silver? What do the men think of this? *While the others were in town, Ben Gunn helped Silver escape, taking a sack of coin worth three or four hundred guineas. Ben Gunn says he helped Silver escape because he felt if he'd stayed aboard, they'd all be killed. Everyone is pleased to be rid of Silver at such a low cost.

4. What are Jim's lingering dreams of the island? Jim dreams of the sound of the surf booming or hearing the cry of Captain Flint, the parrot, saying, "Pieces of eight! pieces of eight!"

Quotations

Identify the speaker of the following.

"You're the man to keep your word, we know that." Dr. Livesey (to Silver)

"Pieces of eight! pieces of eight!" Captain Flint, the parrot (in Jim's dreams)

Discussion Questions

1. Does Dr. Livesey's final comment about the remaining pirates surprise you? What would you have done?
2. Do you think Silver should have gone home free when the remaining crew was marooned?
3. Each man spent his share of the treasure "according to nature." Explain.
   *Ben Gunn is the one who wastes his share of the treasure.
4. Were you satisfied with the ending of *Treasure Island*? How would you have changed the story?

Enrichment

1. Research the following types of coinage Jim sorts through: *moidores*, *sequins.*
2. Write your own alternate ending for *Treasure Island*, going as far back as you wish.

Mastery Word List

derelict/ dereliction **dilapidate** **incense** **rudiment/ rudimentary** **volition**

Synonym Substitution

Write a few good synonyms or a phrase in the blank to replace the highlighted word.

1. His **rudimentary** knowledge of skiing wasn't enough to keep him from falling repeatedly. elementary, simple, beginning, amateur
2. "The true test of a leader is whether his followers will adhere to his cause from their own **volition**, enduring the most arduous hardships without being forced to do so, and remaining steadfast in the moments of greatest peril." - Xenophon free will, choice, decision
3. The child felt **derelict** as the car pulled away without him. abandoned, forgotten, neglected
4. The **rudiments** of learning begin in the home. basics, foundation, building blocks
5. It is unwise to **incense** the gods. anger, enrage
6. Leaving his brother at the pool to go watch a movie with his friends was no minor **dereliction**. act of carelessness, negligence, disregard
7. "I'd rather walk," she said, "than drive around in a **dilapidated** minivan!" tacky, faded, beat-up, decrepit
8. Obedience that is not **volitional** is not obedience. voluntary, willfully chosen

Mastery Substitution

Use a word from the Mastery Word List to replace the highlighted word or phrase.
You may have to change the form of the word to fit the sentence.

1. He was **greatly angered** by the rude words of the driver. incensed
2. This class focuses on teaching the **essential building blocks** of Latin grammar. rudiments
3. All the students were responsible for the **state of ruin** of the classroom. dilapidation
4. Jim got up early and made the family breakfast by his own **free choice**. volition

5. The mother complained that her room had been **neglected** the entire summer. derelict

6. When the "expert" electrician blew the main power supply to the house, Father realized that his knowledge was more **amateurish** than he had advertised. rudimentary

7. Little boys rarely take a bath **voluntarily**. volitionally

9. Everything he owns seems to **fall apart** so quickly. dilapidate

Implementation

Use at least three of the words from the Mastery Word List in a paragraph of your own.

Appendix of Nautical Terms

General Terms

A

abaft—in the direction of the stern
about—on the other tack
adrift—loose from the moorings
alee—when the helm is put over to leeward

B

batten—a thin strip of wood fitted into a pocket in the leach of a fore-and-aft sail to make the sail set better
bear down—to approach from windward
becalmed—said of a vessel when in a calm
belay—to make fast to a pin or cleat
belaying pin—a wooden or iron shape fitting into a rail, and used for securing gear
bilge—the curved part of the ship's hull where the sides and flat bottom meet
bill of exchange—a written agreement in which a debtor agrees to pay a creditor a specified sum on a specified date
boatswain (bosen)—a ship's petty officer in charge of the deck crew, boats, etc.
boom—a spar used for extending the foot of a fore-and-aft sail
bow—the forward part of a vessel's sides
bowsprit—a spar extending out from the stem and carrying the lead of part of the gear for the headsails
breach—seas that break entirely over a vessel
broach—to fly up into the wind unintentionally; to be thrown broadside on, in surf
bulkhead—transverse or longitudinal partition separating portions of the ship
bulwarks—the light plating or wooden extension of the ship's sides above the upper deck
by the board—overboard

C

canted—inclined
capsize—to overturn
capstan—an upright drum around which cables are wound so as to haul them in
capstan bar—a wooden bar used for heaving the capstan by hand
careen—to list or heel over
cat's paw—1. a double-looped knot formed by twisting two bights of rope—the hook of a tackle is passed through them
2. the slight ruffling of the surface of the water caused by passing flaws of wind in calm airs
clamp down—to sprinkle and swab down, as a deck in hot weather
clinch—a half-hitch (knot) stopped to its own part
close-hauled—sailing close to the wind; on the wind, or by the wind
close-reefed—a sail reduced to its smallest area (rolled up)
clove hitch—a bend formed by making two half-hitches about the spar for hitching ratlines to the shrouds
colors—the national ensign (flag)

coxswain (cosen)—the enlisted man in charge of a boat and usually serving as steersman
crossing the line—crossing the Equator

D

Davy Jones' Locker—the bottom of the sea
deadlight—round thick glass in the side of a ship for lighting purposes
dead reckoning—a navigator's reckoning with courses steered and distances run, independent of sights and bearings
derelict—an abandoned vessel at sea
doldrums—the belt on each side of the equator in which little or no wind ordinarily blows
douse—to take in, or lower, a sail; to put out a light; to cover with water
downhaul—a rope led from the head of a headsail and through a block at the foot of the stay for hauling down the sail
draw—a sail when bellied out by the wind
drift—the amount of leeway of a vessel, or of a tide or current

E

ensign—the national flag
even keel—floating level

F

fathom—six feet
fore-and-aft—from the bow to the stern, lengthwise, as in sails
forecastle—the upper deck forward of the foremast
forecastle deck—a partial deck at the bow over the main deck
forefoot—the heel of the stem where it connects to the keel

G

gaff—the spar to which the head of a fore-and-aft sail is secured
galley—the ship's kitchen
gallows—the framework sometimes fitted above the main or superstructure deck for boat stowage and for the stowage of spare parts
gangway—an opening in the bulwarks to give entrance to the ship; or in ships without bulwarks, the opening in the rail used for boarding or leaving the ship
ground swell—the swell encountered in shoal (shallow) water and which is constant
gunwale—the rail of a boat

H

handspike—a small wooden bar similar to a capstan or an anchor bar, used for prying
handy—a handy vessel is one which handles easily
hard-a-lee—to put the tiller all the way up
hatch—an opening in a ship's deck for communication or for handling stores or cargo
hawser—a large rope used for heavy work, such as towing
head—the ship's water closet (bathroom)
helm—the wheel or tiller by which a ship is steered
hold—the space below decks utilized for the stowage of ballast, cargo, and stores (and prisoners)

hulk—a worn-out and stripped vessel
hull—the frame or main body of a ship

J

jib—a headsail set on a stay forward of the foremast
jib-boom—a spar rigged out beyond the bowsprit and through the bowsprit cap
Jolly Roger—a pirate's flag carrying the skull and crossbones

K

keel—the timber or bar forming the backbone of the vessel and running from the stem to the sternpost at the bottom of the ship

L

landing strake—the second line of planking below the gunwale
lanyard—a rope made fast to an article for securing it (e.g., knife lanyard, bucket lanyard) or for setting up rigging
leeward—the direction away from the wind
list—the inclination of a vessel not caused by wind or sea
luff—the forward edge of a fore-and-aft sail
lug—to carry (as to lug sail)
lugger—a sailing vessel with quadrilateral fore-and-aft sails, the head carried on a hoisting yard, and the luff shorter than the leech

M

mainsail—the sail spread by the main gaff and boom
marlinspike—a pointed iron instrument used in working with rope and wire
mast—a vertical spar supporting the booms, gaffs, and sails
masthead—any portion of the upper 15 feet of the lower mast
mizzen—the third mast from forward of a vessel with more than two masts (middle)

N

netting—a rope network

P

pipe to—the boatswain's pipe call to an evolution (or series of tasks)

Q

quartermaster—a petty officer of the bridge force

R

ridgepole—the horizontal pole supporting the middle of an awning
rigging—ropes and chains for a ship's masts and sails
rudder—a flat wooden shape fitted on the sternpost by pintles swivelling in gudgeons, and for the purpose of steering the boat (i.e., the flat board that sits in the back of the boat in the water and steers the boat)

S

schooner—a sailing vessel with two or more masts with fore-and-aft sails and with head sails carried on a bowsprit and jib-boom
scud—low-lying mist clouds
scull—to propel a boat by working an oar from side to side over the stern
scuttle-butt—the container of fresh water for drinking purposes and used by the crew; formerly it consisted of a cask
sea-cock—a cock in a pipe connected to the sea; a vessel may be flooded by opening the sea-cock
sheet—the rope used to spread the clew of headsails and to control the boom of boom sails
shipping articles—the agreement of the ship's officers and the crew with the owners or agents (sign articles)
shipshape—neat, seamanlike
shore up—to prop up
shove off—to leave
shrouds—side stays of hemp or wire from the masthead to the rail and set up by dead-eyes
slip—to let go by unshackling, as of a cable
smart—snappy, seamanlike (a smart ship is an efficient one)
spar—a slender rod or pole (as a mast) supporting the sail of a ship
spyglass—a small hand telescope
stanchions—wooden or metal uprights used as supports
stern—the rear end of a ship
stern sheets—the space in a boat abaft the afterthwart
stow—to put in place
supercargo—a merchant vessel's officer charged with managing the ship's business

T

tack—to change from one tack to another by putting the helm down; close-hauled on the wind
tarpaulin—heavy canvas used as a covering
taut—with no slack; strict as to discipline
teeth—directly towards the wind
thwart—a seat across a boat on which a rower may sit
tiller—a short piece of iron or wood fitting into the rudder head and by which the rudder is turned
topmast—the mast next above the lower mast
top sides—above deck

W

weather—to windward
weather eye—(to keep a weather eye is to be on the alert)
weather gauge—the situation of a vessel to windward of another vessel
wide berth—at a considerable distance
windward—toward the wind

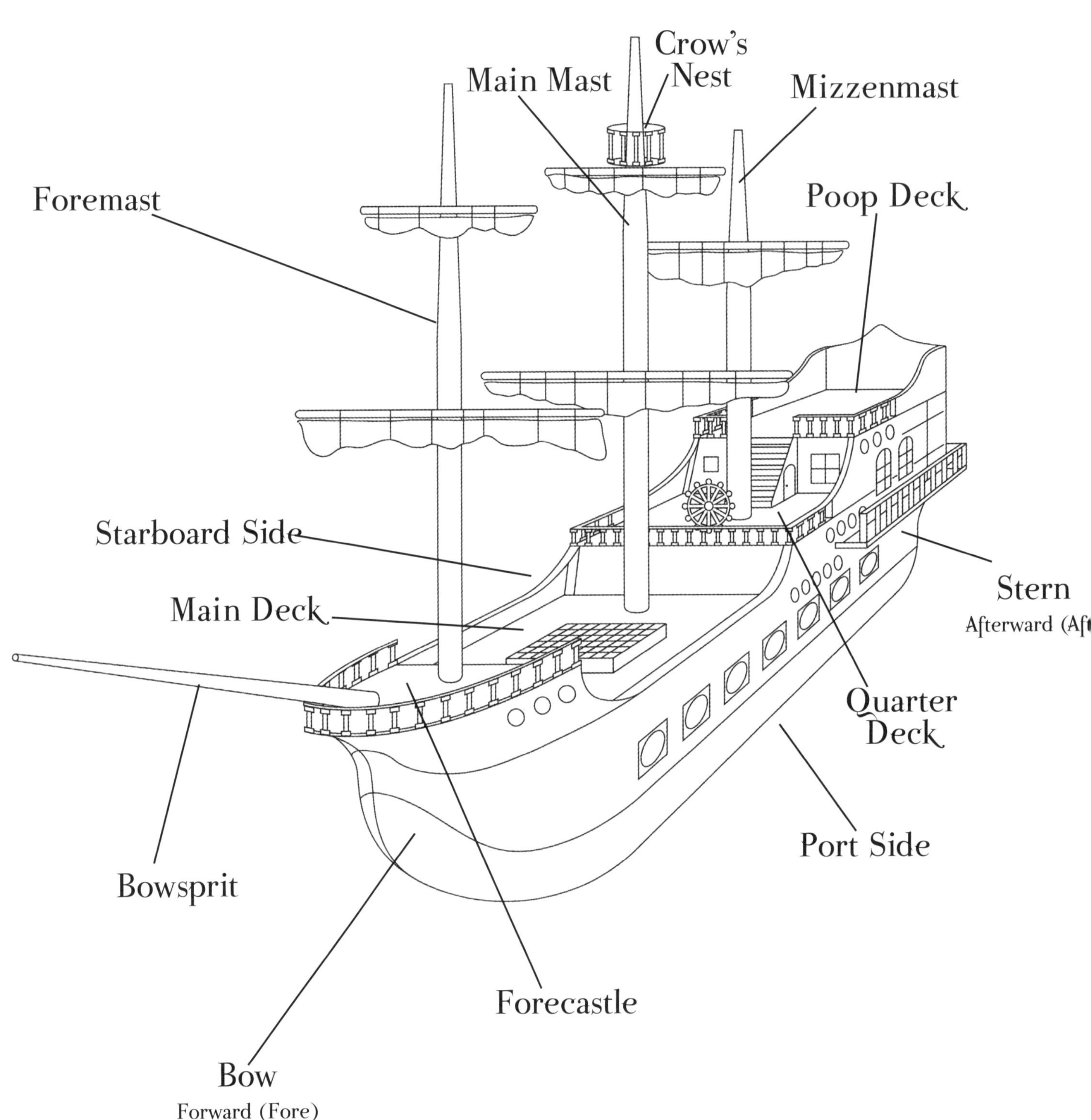
Crow's Nest
Main Mast
Mizzenmast
Foremast
Poop Deck
Starboard Side
Main Deck
Stern
Afterward (Af
Quarter Deck
Port Side
Bowsprit
Forecastle
Bow
Forward (Fore)

Parts of a Ship

bow—the forward part of a vessel's sides
bridge—a crosswise platform or enclosed area above the main deck of a ship from which the ship is controlled
brig—the ship's prison, formerly a sailor's slang phrase
cabin—the captain's quarters
crow's nest—the platform on the mast for the lookout
forecastle—the upper deck forward of the foremast
galley—the ship's kitchen
gallows—the framework sometimes fitted above the main or superstructure deck for boat stowage and for the stowage of spare parts
gunwale—the rail of a boat
head—the ship's water closet (bathroom)
helm—the wheel or tiller by which a ship is steered
hold—the space below decks utilized for storage
magazine—the space provided for the stowage of explosives
mast—a tall vertical pole (spar) used to support the sails and yards (horizontal poles) on a ship
rudder—a broad, flat, moveable piece hinged to the rear of a ship, used for steering
skids—beams sometimes fitted over the decks for the stowage of heavy boats
spar—a slender pole or rod supporting the sail of a ship
steerage—the junior officer's quarters
stern—the rear part of a ship
tiller—a short piece of iron or wood fitting into the rudder head and by which the rudder is turned
uptake—the enclosed trunk connecting a boiler or a group of boilers to the smoke stack

Sails and Parts of Sails

batten—a thin strip of wood fitted into a pocket in the leach of a fore-and-aft sail to make the sail set better
clew—the after lower corner of a fore-and-aft sail
foot—the lower edge of a sail
jib—a headsail set on a stay forward of the foremast
luff—the forward edge of a fore-and-aft sail
mainsail—the sail spread by the main gaff and boom
rigging—the ropes and chains for a vessel's masts and sails
tack—the lower forward corner of a fore-and-aft sail
topsail—a sail set over a lower sail
yard—a light spar to which the head of a lug rig sail is secured; in a square-rigged vessel, the spar suspended horizontally from the mast and to which the head of a square sail is bent

Boats and Ships

derelict—an abandoned vessel at sea
gig—a ship's boat designated for the use of a commanding officer
hulk—a worn-out and stripped vessel
lugger—a sailing vessel with quadrilateral fore-and-aft sails, the head carried on a hoisting yard, and the luff shorter than the leech
jolly boat—a small boat used in the merchant service and corresponding to a dinghy on a man-of-war
punt—a rectangular flat-bottomed boat, usually propelled by sculling and used for cleaning and painting the water line
schooner—a sailing vessel with two or more masts, with fore-and-aft sails and with head sails carried on a bowsprit and jib-boom

Ropes and Knots

bowline—a hitch in the form of a noose; used for securing hawsers to decks or moorings, and for lowering men over the side of a ship, etc.
cable—a rope; a chain secured to an anchor
cat's paw—a type of knot; a double-loop formed by twisting two bights of rope—the hook of a tackle is passed through them
clinch—a half-hitch (knot) stopped to its own part
clove hitch—a knot formed by making two half-hitches about the spar for hitching ratlines to the shrouds
cordage—a general term for rope of all kinds
hawser—a large rope used for heavy work, such as towing
junk—old rope
ratline stuff—small stuff (rope), three-stranded, right-handed, and tarred; used for rattling rigging
spun yarn—rough stuff made from long tow, laid up loosely left-handed of two, three, or four strands; used for seizings and small stuff
thrums—short strands of rope with strands unlaid and stuck through a mat to make a rough surface
yarn—1. twisted fibers (for rope) 2. tales—to "spin a yarn" is to tell a story

Wind and Sea, Directions, and Sailing Terms

abaft—by
about—on the other tack (or direction)
alee—when the helm is put over to leeward
all-aback—when all the sails are in stays (heavy rope or cable)
becalmed—said of a vessel when in a calm (no wind)
breach—seas that break entirely over a vessel
cat's paw—the slight ruffling of the surface of the water caused by passing flaws of wind in calm airs
close-hauled—sailing close to the wind
close-reefed—a sail reduced to its smallest area (rolled up)
draw—a sail when bellied out by the wind
drift—the amount of leeway of a vessel, or of a tide or current
fore-and-aft—from the bow to the stern, lengthwise, as in sails
full spread—having all sails set
furl—to gather up and secure a sail
ground swell—the swell encountered in shoal (shallow) water and which is constant
hand—to furl a sail
haul to windward—to bring a vessel to the wind when sailing free
head to wind—the situation of a vessel in the eye of the wind
heave to—to bring a vessel's head to the wind and hold her there by the use of the sails
in stays—the situation of a vessel when coming about and the wind is spilled from the sails
larboard—port; left
leeward—away from the wind; the side or direction away from the wind
lie—the same as "heave to"
luff her—an order to bring the vessel into the wind by putting the helm down
mend—to refurl a sail which has been improperly furled
port—the left side of a ship; to turn the helm to the port side; an opening in the ship
scudding—driving before a gale
starboard—to steer right; right side of the ship
trades—the practically steady winds found in the Tropics and blowing towards the Equator
teeth—directly towards or into the wind
weather tide—a tide setting to windward
windward—towards the wind; the side or direction from which the wind blows

Discussion Questions
Answer Key

(Not every chapter's Discussion Questions require a key, nor every Discussion Question within a chapter. These questions have been left out of the key.)

Chapter 1 & Chapter 2

4. What was Dr. Livesey's advice to the captain? Do you agree with this advice?

    Dr. Livesey's advice to the captain was to quit drinking rum or it would be the death of him.

Chapter 3

1. What is the "black spot"?

    The "black spot" consists of a piece of paper with one side blackened. It is presented to someone to officially pronounce a verdict of guilt or judgment. It was a source of fear because it meant the person was to be deposed as leader, by force if necessary, or even killed.

2. What does the captain mean when he says rum has been "meat and drink, and man and wife" to him?

    The captain means rum has been a comfort to him, all he needs in life to be content.

Chapter 4

1. Why does Jim call his mother both "honest and greedy"? Do you agree with him?

    Jim's mother is portrayed as both honest and greedy in that she is not willing to take more than is due her from the captain's chest, but she is also not willing to settle for any less, even though the inn is about to be invaded.

Chapter 5

2. What is "Flint's fist"?

    Flint's fist is the oilskin packet containing the treasure map.

Chapter 7

2. What does Trelawney mean when he describes Long John Silver as "a man of substance"?

    He most likely means he believes Silver to be a man of strong character, reliable and capable.

Chapter 10

1. What does Silver mean when he says, "You can't touch pitch and not be mucked"?

    He means that when you are around a vulgar life, you are bound to take on vulgar ways, whether you are aware of it or not. He is referring to the bad language his parrot has acquired from his days at sea with pirates.

Chapter 11

1. What is a "gentleman of fortune"?

    a common pirate

2. What does the phrase "Dead men don't bite" mean?

    The phrase means that if they kill the crew, then the crew won't be able to cause trouble for them later.

Chapter 12

1. What does the captain mean when he says Silver would "look remarkably well from a yard-arm"?

    A yard is a spar on a mast from which sails are set; a yard-arm is the outermost tips of the yard. The captain means he wants to see Silver hanged from this spot.

Chapter 13

1. The doctor says he smells fever on the island, and the whole crew seems to have caught the "infection" of mutiny. Why does the author so closely use the analogies of fever and infection when referring to Treasure Island?

   The author uses these analogies to show the effect money can have on people; greed can practically possess people and make them do things they wouldn't normally do, as though they are taken over by a sickness.

Chapter 14

1. To which animals does the author/Jim compare Silver? What other words are used in the place of Silver's name, labeling him? What effect does this have on the reader?

   He compares Silver to a snake, then a monkey. Instead of using Silver's name, the author calls him "the monster" and "the murderer." This lets the reader know how strongly Jim feels about the cruelty of the situation, and allows the reader to identify with Jim more when they see Silver through his eyes.

Chapter 15

1. Ben Gunn believes that Providence put him there on the island. What does he mean by this? Do you agree with him?

   Ben means that he was meant to be marooned on the island because now he is good and pious, where he wasn't before.

Chapter 16

2. What does the incident between Smollett and Gray further reveal about Smollett's character?

   The incident reveals that Smollett is willing to take chances on men he believes are truly good and that can benefit his cause. It shows he is brave and hopeful.

Chapter 17 & Chapter 18

2. Redruth is described as laying "like a Trojan" behind his mattress. What is meant by this reference?

   The Trojans were strong, mighty warriors. To compare Redruth to one meant he was fighting with great determination and zeal.

Chapter 19

1. What is the Jolly Roger? What is the Union Jack? What is their significance?

   The Jolly Roger is the skull and crossbones black flag of pirates, while the Union Jack is the British flag. Each flag represents the group's unwillingness to surrender and stands as a threat to the opposing group.

2. What does it mean that the doctor "staked his wig"?

   When the doctor "staked his wig" it meant that he metaphorically bet his wig that the mutineers would soon be sick from the climate.

Chapter 25

2. Why does Jim say, "Better none than these" when taking down the Jolly Roger?

   Jim means that it would be better to have no flag (colors) waving at all than to have the pirates' flag (colors) waving, since the flag represents allegiance to the pirates' way.

Chapter 26

1. How does Jim know that the coxswain is lying when he says he prefers wine to brandy?

   Jim knows Israel Hands is lying because his eyes never meet his, he wanders about with eyes going to and fro, and he keeps smiling and "putting his tongue out in the most guilty, embarrassed manner, so that a child could have told that he was bent on some deception."

Chapter 27

1. Which apprehensions should Jim have heeded when heading back to camp?

   He should have inspected the fire glowing in the sky, and not assumed that the snoring from the camp was from his friends, since he was alerted by the large fire that something was different. The pecking of Silver's parrot should also have been a clue.

2. Where do you think Jim's friends are?

   Jim's friends are most likely the ones that lit the fire in the sky, as a signal to Jim.

Chapter 29

1. What was Silver trying to do by pointing out the fact that the men had used a page from the Bible to deliver the black spot?

   Silver was trying to sow doubt in their minds by pointing out that they used a page from the Bible, and no good could come of that.

Chapter 30

1. Why does the doctor tell Jim, "There is a kind of fate in this"? Do you agree?

   The doctor believes that Jim keeps saving their lives with each move he makes, intentional or not.

Chapter 31

1. What does living "hand to mouth" mean?

   It means living without planning for tomorrow, using the resources one has just to get through the present day.

Chapter 33

1. Who is the chieftain the chapter title refers to?

   The chapter title refers to Silver.

2. What does the squire mean when he says the dead men hang about Silver's neck like millstones?

   A millstone is a metaphor for a heavy weight or burden, meaning that Silver will not easily forget his evil deeds.

Quizzes & Final Test

(reproducible for classroom use)

Quiz 1

Chapters 1-6

Name ______________________________

Date ______________________________

Vocabulary: Supply the Mastery Word that makes the most sense in the sentence. Make sure to use the correct form.

condescend connoisseur formidable miscreant repugnance

1. When he took the trash out, the smell was so ____________________ (adj.) that he almost felt sick.
2. Your __________________ (adj.) attitude does not make people want to do what you ask.
3. They always let Cody pick the movie when they went to the theater since he considered himself a movie __________________ (n.).
4. A squirrel had gotten into our attic, and the little __________________ (n.) chewed holes in our wiring.
5. The huge player moved _____________________ (adv.) down the field.

Bonus:

1. Although the professor was brilliant, he could be quite __________________ (adj.) when it came to his schedule.
2. Although the Henson family was all very well behaved, they all could be guilty of ___________________ (adj.) when it came to who got the last cookie.

Who Said It?: Circle the correct speaker of the quote given.

1. "I'm a plain man; rum and bacon and eggs is what I want."

   a. Dr. Livesey
   b. Jim Hawkins
   c. The captain/Billy Bones
   d. Jim's mother
   e. Squire Trelawney
   f. the blind beggar

2. "If I can't see, I can hear a finger stirring."

   a. Dr. Livesey
   b. Jim Hawkins
   c. The captain/Billy Bones
   d. Jim's mother
   e. Squire Trelawney
   f. the blind beggar

3. "I'll have my dues, and not a farthing over."

   a. Dr. Livesey
   b. Jim Hawkins
   c. The captain/Billy Bones
   d. Jim's mother
   e. Squire Trelawney
   f. the blind beggar

4. "I believe I have the thing in my breast-pocket."

a. Dr. Livesey
b. Jim Hawkins
c. The captain/Billy Bones
d. Jim's mother
e. Squire Trelawney
f. the blind beggar

5. "I'll be as silent as the grave."

a. Dr. Livesey
b. Jim Hawkins
c. The captain/Billy Bones
d. Jim's mother
e. Squire Trelawney
f. the blind beggar

Multiple Choice: Circle the correct answer.

1. Who haunted Jim's dreams?

a. the captain/Billy Bones
b. the man with one leg
c. Jim's father
d. Black Dog

2. What was the captain's reaction to seeing Black Dog?

a. happy
b. sickened
c. surprised
d. both b and c

3. Who or what caused the death of the captain/Billy Bones?

a. Captain Flint
b. the blind beggar
c. Black Dog
d. the black spot

4. What did Jim's mother call the neighboring people after she asked them for help?

a. chicken-hearted
b. heroes
c. yellow
d. brave

5. According to Pew, who else was involved in the plot?

a. Captain Flint
b. Captain Bones
c. Black Dog
d. the man with one leg

6. What did Jim think the beggar and his men were looking for at the inn?

a. money
b. the black spot
c. Flint's fist
d. revenge on Captain Bones

7. What was in the oilskin packet?

a. gold
b. a treasure map
c. tobacco
d. all of the above

8. Why was the doctor hesitant to join the expedition?

a. He feared the squire wouldn't keep it a secret.
b. He didn't believe there was a hidden treasure.
c. He didn't want to put Jim in danger.
d. He was afraid for his own life.

Quiz 2

Chapters 7-11

Name ____________________

Date ____________________

Vocabulary: Supply the Mastery Word that makes the most sense in the sentence. Make sure to use the correct form.

brood   derisive   dexterity/dexterous   mirth   slight

1. The bully laughed ______________________ (adv.) at his classmate.
2. "It is not by muscle, speed, or physical ______________________ (n.) that great things are achieved, but by reflection, force of character, and judgment." – Cicero
3. "Meat eaten without either ______________________ (n.) or music is of ill digestion." – Sir Walter Scott
4. There she sat, ______________________ (v.) over her lost purse.
5. The worker felt ______________________ (adj.) when they gave the promotion to someone else.

Bonus:

1. The stubborn child would not ______________________(v.) his sister's stolen toy.
2. Defeat after defeat could not dampen the ______________________ (adj.) spirit of the little league's last place team.

Who Said It?: Circle the correct speaker of the quote given.

1. "Imagine the abominable age we live in!"

   a. Dr. Livesey
   b. Jim Hawkins
   c. Long John Silver
   d. Israel Hands
   e. Squire Trelawney
   f. Captain Smollett

2. "You're as smart as paint."

   a. Dr. Livesey
   b. Jim Hawkins
   c. Long John Silver
   d. Israel Hands
   e. Squire Trelawney
   f. Captain Smollet

3. "I don't like this cruise; I don't like the men; and I don't like my officer. That's short and sweet."

   a. Dr. Livesey
   b. Jim Hawkins
   c. Long John Silver
   d. Israel Hands
   e. Squire Trelawney
   f. Captain Smollet

4. "A trifle more of that man, and I should explode."

a. Dr. Livesey
b. Jim Hawkins
c. Long John Silver
d. Israel Hands
e. Squire Trelawney
f. Captain Smollet

5. "Dooty is dooty, mates. I give my vote—death."

a. Dr. Livesey
b. Jim Hawkins
c. Long John Silver
d. Israel Hands
e. Squire Trelawney
f. Captain Smollet

Multiple Choice: Circle the correct answer.

1. What in the squire's letter did Jim think the doctor would not like?

a. The squire spent too much money on the ship.
b. The cook the squire hired only had one leg.
c. The squire told people in Bristol about the treasure.
d. The squire said Jim could spend only one night with his mother.

2. Why did Jim cry before leaving home?

a. His mother hired an apprentice boy to take Jim's place.
b. He missed his father.
c. He was afraid of leaving home on a dangerous mission.
d. He didn't get to say goodbye to his mother.

3. What was Jim's overall impression of Long John Silver after meeting him?

a. Jim was suspicious of Silver.
b. Jim was afraid of Silver.
c. Jim thought Silver was bad-tempered.
d. Jim felt comfortable with Silver.

4. Who did the squire call "unmanly, unsailorly, and downright un-English"?

a. Captain Smollett
b. Long John Silver
c. Mr. Arrow
d. Israel Hands

5. What happened to Mr. Arrow?

a. He stole the treasure map.
b. He disappeared.
c. He was killed by someone on board.
d. He got violently ill.

6. What did Captain Smollett admit?

a. The crew was well-behaved.
b. He still disliked the cruise.
c. He fancied the ship itself.
d. all of the above

7. What did Dick ask Silver about the plan?

a. He asked how much treasure he would get.
b. He asked what to do with the crew afterwards.
c. He asked not to be killed.
d. He asked where the treasure was.

8. Who did Silver want to kill himself?

a. Captain Smollett
b. Dr. Livesey
c. Squire Trelawney
d. Jim

Quiz 3

Chapters 12-16

Name ______________________________

Date ______________________________

Vocabulary: Supply the Mastery Word that makes the most sense in the sentence. Make sure to use the correct form.

duplicity extricate qualm

1. The magician was able to deftly ________________(v.) himself from the straightjacket.
2. The longer the politician spoke, the more ________________(adj.) his words sounded.
3. Brett had no ____________________(n.) with taking the last doughnut.

Bonus:

1. The teacher felt that somehow break dancing was ____________________(adv.) with Latin recitation.
2. Scott thought the heat wasn't merely inconvenient, it was down-right ______________(adj.).

Who Said It?: Circle the correct speaker of the quote given.

1. "And to think that they're all Englishmen! Sir, I could find it in my heart to blow the ship up."

a. Dr. Livesey
b. Tom
c. Long John Silver
d. Ben Gunn
e. Squire Trelawney
f. Captain Smollett

2. "I don't know about treasure, but I'll stake my wig there's fever here."

a. Dr. Livesey
b. Tom
c. Long John Silver
d. Ben Gunn
e. Squire Trelawney
f. Captain Smollett

3. "If I die like a dog, I'll die in my duty."

a. Dr. Livesey
b. Tom
c. Long John Silver
d. Ben Gunn
e. Squire Trelawney
f. Captain Smollett

4. "If you was sent by Long John, I'm as good as pork, and I know it."

a. Dr. Livesey
b. Tom
c. Long John Silver
d. Ben Gunn
e. Squire Trelawney
f. Captain Smollett

5. "I know you are a good man at bottom, and I daresay not one of the lot of you's as bad as he makes out."

a. Dr. Livesey
b. Tom
c. Long John Silver
d. Ben Gunn
e. Squire Trelawney
f. Captain Smollett

Multiple Choice: Circle the correct answer.

1. What surprised Jim most about Silver?

a. how he could move about so quickly on one leg
b. how he was planning to murder everyone to keep the treasure for himself
c. how cool he was while giving information about the island
d. how nice he was

2. Why did the squire, doctor, and captain feel Jim could help them more than anyone else?

a. Jim was a good liar.
b. The crew was open with Jim.
c. Silver trusted Jim.
d. Jim knew where to find the treasure.

3. Who was the "one man to rely on" for our heroes?

a. Jim
b. Long John Silver
c. Ben Gunn
d. Captain Smollett

4. What was Jim's initial emotion after escaping onto the island?

a. fear for his safety
b. relief to stretch his legs
c. regret for leaving his friends behind
d. joy to explore the island

5. Who was the victim of "The First Blow"?

a. Jim b. Tom c. Silver d. Alan

6. What did Ben Gunn want from Jim?

a. to be left alone
b. the treasure map
c. cheese
d. all of the above

7. According to Ben Gunn, who put him there on the island?

a. Captain Flint b. Providence c. Long John Silver d. the devil

8. Who among the crew did Captain Smollett risk his life for?

a. Abraham Gray
b. Joyce
c. Hunter
d. Dick

Quiz 4

Chapters 17-24

Name ______________________________

Date ______________________________

Vocabulary: Supply the Mastery Word that makes the most sense in the sentence. Make sure to use the correct form.

acquiesce   infallible   flourish   callous

1. Andrew wondered how his father could be so __________________(adj.) as to not let him get the new video game.
2. The salesman ____________________(v.) at his new job.
3. After he explained his position clearly, his friend finally ________________________(v.) to the truth.
4. "The wise know too well their weakness to assume ______________________(n.); and he who knows most, knows best how little he knows." - Thomas Jefferson

Bonus:

1. The angry prisoner hurled _________________________ (n.) at his jailers.
2. Tanya found it difficult to ______________________ (v.) her son's motive when he brought her candy.

Who Said It?: Circle the correct speaker of the quote given.

1. "Strike my colors! No, sir, not I."

   a. Abraham Gray
   b. Jim Hawkins
   c. Long John Silver
   d. Ben Gunn
   e. Squire Trelawney
   f. Captain Smollett

2. "You're a good boy, or I'm mistook; but you're only a boy, all told."

   a. Abraham Gray
   b. Jim Hawkins
   c. Long John Silver
   d. Ben Gunn
   e. Squire Trelawney
   f. Captain Smollett

3. "Laugh, by thunder, laugh! Before an hour's out, ye'll laugh upon the other side. Them that die'll be the lucky ones."

   a. Abraham Gray
   b. Jim Hawkins
   c. Long John Silver
   d. Ben Gunn
   e. Squire Trelawney
   f. Captain Smollett

4. "Well, shipmate, mad he may not be; but if *he's* not, you mark my words, *I* am!"

a. Abraham Gray
b. Jim Hawkins
c. Long John Silver
d. Ben Gunn
e. Squire Trelawney
f. Captain Smollett

5. "Clumsy fellows, they must still be drunk as owls."

a. Abraham Gray
b. Jim Hawkins
c. Long John Silver
d. Ben Gunn
e. Squire Trelawney
f. Captain Smollett

Multiple Choice: Circle the correct answer.

1. Who was the first of Captain Smollett's men to die?

a. Hunter
b. Joyce
c. Redruth
d. Gray

2. What did Captain Smollett insist on doing?

a. hanging the British flag
b. hanging the Jolly Roger
c. searching for Jim
d. burying their man

3. What was the group's "best hope" for survival?

a. finding the treasure
b. killing all the mutineers
c. sending Ben Gunn as a messenger
d. hiding in the woods

4. What did Captain Smollett do when Silver came to seek a truce?

a. He handed over a fake treasure map.
b. He told Silver he'd take his men back to England for a fair trial.
c. He offered to give the mutineers all their provisions.
d. He shot one of Silver's men.

5. What was the price of the heroes' victory?

a. Joyce died.
b. Hunter died.
c. Jim was taken hostage.
d. They lost all their provisions.

6. Where did Jim think the doctor was going when he left camp?

a. to find the treasure
b. to talk to Silver
c. to see Ben Gunn
d. to find the Hispaniola

7. What was Jim's plan?

a. kill Silver in his sleep
b. cut the Hispaniola adrift
c. find Ben Gunn
d. steal back their provisions

8. How did Jim react to his impending doom in the coracle?

a. He began to cry.
b. He jumped overboard.
c. He cried out for help.
d. He was resigned to his death.

Quiz 5

Chapters 25-29

Name ______________________

Date ______________________

Vocabulary: Supply the Mastery Word that makes the most sense in the sentence. Make sure to use the correct form.

volition dilapidate incense

1. The boys all dared each other to go into the old, ____________________ (adj.) house.
2. It does no good to simply exercise ____________________ (n.); you need to make sure you do what is right.
3. The baby was ____________________ (v.) by the loss of the toy.

Bonus:

1. "Remember that there is nothing stable in human affairs; therefore avoid undue ____________________ (n.) in prosperity, or undue depression in adversity." – Socrates
2. The ____________________ (adj.) crowd demanded that the gold be returned to them.

Who Said It?: Circle the correct speaker of the quote given.

1. "I don't have no manner of luck, you see, and that's what's the matter with me."

   a. George Merry
   b. Jim Hawkins
   c. Long John Silver
   d. Israel Hands
   e. Squire Trelawney
   f. Captain Smollett

2. "You can kill the body, Mr. Hands, but not the spirit; you must know that already."

   a. George Merry
   b. Jim Hawkins
   c. Long John Silver
   d. Israel Hands
   e. Squire Trelawney
   f. Captain Smollett

3. "Pieces of eight! pieces of eight!"

   a. George Merry
   b. Silver's parrot
   c. Long John Silver
   d. Israel Hands
   e. Job Anderson
   f. Morgan

4. "The laugh's on my side; I've had the top of this business from the first."

   a. George Merry
   b. Jim Hawkins
   c. Long John Silver
   d. Israel Hands
   e. Squire Trelawney
   f. Captain Smollett

5. "The black spot! I thought so."

   a. George Merry
   b. Jim Hawkins
   c. Long John Silver
   d. Israel Hands
   e. Squire Trelawney
   f. Captain Smollett

Multiple Choice: Circle the correct answer.

1. What did the coxswain do for Jim in exchange for food, drink, and a bandaged leg?

   a. He promised not to kill Jim.
   b. He promised to share the treasure.
   c. He showed Jim how to sail.
   d. He agreed to join Jim and his men.

2. How did Jim find out that the coxswain was planning to kill him?

   a. The coxswain told him this plan.
   b. Jim saw him hide a knife in his coat.
   c. Jim overheard him tell a crew mate.
   d. The coxswain was not planning to kill Jim.

3. What weakness in Jim was almost his downfall?

   a. cockiness
   b. fear
   c. suspicion
   d. his physical inferiority

4. As Jim neared the camp, what put him at ease?

   a. the sight of the camp fire
   b. the sound of Silver's parrot
   c. the smell of food cooking
   d. the sound of his friends snoring

5. How did Jim respond when Silver asked him to choose a side?

   a. Jim demanded to know where his friends were.
   b. Jim cried and begged Silver to spare his life.
   c. Jim said he would not defend Silver in court.
   d. Jim admitted to everything he'd done since overhearing them in the apple barrel.

6. What did Silver reveal to Jim was in his possession?

   a. the treasure map
   b. the treasure
   c. Ben Gunn
   d. the Hispaniola

7. What did the buccaneers bring back to Silver?

   a. food
   b. weapons
   c. the black spot
   d. the Hispaniola

8. As Jim fell asleep, for whom did he feel sorry?

   a. Silver
   b. himself
   c. Israel Hands
   d. Ben Gunn

Final Exam

Chapters 1-34

Name ____________________

Date ____________________

Vocabulary:

Supply the Mastery Word that makes the most sense in the sentence. Make sure to use the correct form. Use the words in the first list to answer questions 1-8 and the second list for 9-15.

acquiesce	derelict	dilapidate	extricate
incense	qualm	rudiment	volition

1. The employee was fired because he was constantly ____________________(adj.) in his duty.
2. A ____________________(adj.) understanding of physics is needed to build a catapult.
3. After many months of deliberation, the two parties finally ____________________(v.) to the plan suggested by the representative.
4. Her parents were surprised to see that she made her bed of her own ____________________(n.).
5. The Greek was ____________________(v.) by the enemy's mistreatment of the temple of Athena, and he called down imprecations against them.
6. Years of misuse had left the bridge ____________________(adj.) and not safe to cross.
7. Uncomfortable with large groups of people, he sought to ____________________(v.) himself from the crowd.
8. Paris believed that Helen rightfully belonged to him, so he had no ____________________(n.) in stealing her from Menelaus.

callous	duplicity	flourish	formidable
grapple	infallible	mirth	

9. The student won the debate by his ____________________(adj.) use of logic.
10. The garden ____________________(v.) under her attentive care.
11. When they got to the base of the mountain, the idea of climbing it seemed far more ____________________(adj.) than it did the day before.
12. "You may have all the solemnity you wish in your neckties, but in anything important you must have ____________________(n.) or you will have madness." - G. K. Chesterton
13. The boy cried "wolf!" so many times that the townspeople had grown ____________________(adj.) to his cries.
14. When she came home with her driver's permit, her parents were forced to ____________________(v.) with the idea that their little girl was growing up.
15. The honest and true judge was never guilty of ____________________(n.).

Who Said It?: Circle the correct speaker of the quote given.

1. "There is a kind of fate in this."

   a. Dr. Livesey
   b. Jim Hawkins
   c. Long John Silver
   d. George Merry
   e. Squire Trelawney
   f. Captain Smollett

2. "We'll save our necks in spite of fate and fortune."

   a. Dr. Livesey
   b. Jim Hawkins
   c. Long John Silver
   d. George Merry
   e. Squire Trelawney
   f. Captain Smollett

3. "Fetch aft the rum, Darby!"

   a. Dr. Livesey
   b. Silver's parrot
   c. Long John Silver
   d. George Merry
   e. the ghost of Captain Flint
   f. Ben Gunn

4. "But the dead men, sir, hang about your neck like millstones."

   a. Dr. Livesey
   b. Jim Hawkins
   c. Long John Silver
   d. George Merry
   e. Squire Trelawney
   f. Captain Smollett

5. "You're the man to keep your word, we know that."

   a. Dr. Livesey
   b. Jim Hawkins
   c. Long John Silver
   d. George Merry
   e. Squire Trelawney
   f. Captain Smollett

6. "I'll be as silent as the grave."

   a. Dr. Livesey
   b. Jim Hawkins
   c. The captain/Billy Bones
   d. Jim's mother
   e. Squire Trelawney
   f. Pew/the blind beggar

7. "You're as smart as paint."

   a. Dr. Livesey
   b. Jim Hawkins
   c. Long John Silver
   d. Israel Hands
   e. Squire Trelawney
   f. Captain Smollet

8. "I know you are a good man at bottom, and I daresay not one of the lot of you's as bad as he makes out."

   a. Dr. Livesey
   b. Tom
   c. Long John Silver
   d. Ben Gunn
   e. Squire Trelawney
   f. Captain Smollett

9. "Strike my colors! No, sir, not I."

   a. Abraham Gray
   b. Jim Hawkins
   c. Long John Silver
   d. Ben Gunn
   e. Squire Trelawney
   f. Captain Smollett

10. "The laugh's on my side; I've had the top of this business from the first."

a. George Merry
b. Jim Hawkins
c. Long John Silver
d. Israel Hands
e. Squire Trelawney
f. Captain Smollett

Multiple Choice: Circle the correct answer.

1. Who or what caused the death of the captain/Billy Bones?

a. Captain Flint
b. the blind beggar
c. Black Dog
d. the black spot

2. What did Jim think the beggar and his men were looking for at the inn?

a. money
b. the black spot
c. Flint's fist
d. revenge on Captain Bones

3. What was Jim's overall impression of Long John Silver after meeting him?

a. Jim was suspicious of Silver.
b. Jim was afraid of Silver.
c. Jim thought Silver was bad-tempered.
d. Jim felt comfortable with Silver.

4. Who did the squire initially loathe?

a. Captain Smollett
b. Long John Silver
c. Mr. Arrow
d. Israel Hands

5. Why did the squire, doctor, and captain feel Jim could help them more than anyone else?

a. Jim was a good liar.
b. The crew was open with Jim.
c. Silver trusted Jim.
d. Jim knew where to find the treasure.

6. Who was the victim of "The First Blow"?

a. Jim b. Tom c. Silver d. Alan

7. What did Captain Smollett insist on doing?

a. hanging the British flag
b. hanging the Jolly Roger
c. searching for Jim
d. burying their man

8. What was the group's "best hope" for survival?

a. finding the treasure
b. killing all the mutineers
c. sending Ben Gunn as a messenger
d. hiding in the woods

9. How did Jim find out that the coxswain was planning to kill him?

a. The coxswain told him this plan.
b. Jim saw him hide a knife in his coat.
c. Jim overheard him tell a crew mate.
d. The coxswain was not planning to kill Jim.

10. What weakness in Jim was almost his downfall against Israel Hands?

a. cockiness
b. fear
c. suspicion
d. his physical inferiority

11. What was Flint's pointer?

a. a very tall tree
b. a pirate's skeleton
c. a pickaxe
d. a pointy rock

12. What were Captain Flint's last words?

a. "Darby M'Graw!"
b. "Pieces of eight! pieces of eight!"
c. "Shiver me timbers!"
d. "Fetch aft the rum, Darby!"

13. Whose was the voice the pirates heard?

a. Ben Gunn
b. Jim
c. Captain Flint
d. Dr. Livesey

14. What became of Silver?

a. He was left on the island to die.
b. He jumped overboard on the trip back.
c. He was hanged on the gallows.
d. He escaped with a sack of coins.

15. Who wasted his share of the treasure?

a. Jim
b. Squire Trelawney
c. Ben Gunn
d. Captain Smollett

Characters: Match the following characters with their correct description.

1. ___ Jim Hawkins
2. ___ Captain Smollett
3. ___ Dr. Livesey
4. ___ Squire Trelawney
5. ___ Long John Silver
6. ___ Israel Hands
7. ___ Tom Morgan
8. ___ Black Dog
9. ___ Billy Bones
10. ___ Mr. Arrow
11. ___ Tom Redruth
12. ___ George Merry
13. ___ Pew
14. ___ Captain Flint
15. ___ Ben Gunn
16. ___ Abraham Gray

A. old pirate with a scar on his cheek; given the black spot
B. blind beggar; delivered the black spot
C. pirate missing two fingers; visited the Admiral Benbow Inn
D. seen drinking at the Spy-glass tavern; wanted to kill Jim
E. narrated part of the story; gave treatment to sick men
F. the ship's mate; a drunk; disappeared one night
G. landowner who financed the treasure hunt expedition
H. the gamekeeper; the first casualty of our heroes
I. maroon living on the island for three years
J. the ship's cook; double-dealing one-legged pirate
K. the ship's coxswain; Jim killed him
L. captain of the ship; became quite a hero
M. originally a mutineer; joined the captain and his men
N. infamous pirate; buried treasure on an island
O. narrator of most of the story; young boy
P. buccaneer with yellow eyes; accused Silver of ruining the trip

Essay: Answer the following question on the lines provided.

Who do you think was the greatest hero of *Treasure Island*: Jim Hawkins, Captain Smollett, Ben Gunn, or someone else? Give detailed evidence from the book to support your choice.

Quiz & Final Test Keys

Quiz 1 Answer Key

Chapters 1-6

Name ______________________

Date ______________________

Vocabulary: Supply the Mastery Word that makes the most sense in the sentence. Make sure to use the correct form.

condescend connoisseur formidable miscreant repugnance

1. When he took the trash out, the smell was so ___repugnant___ (adj.) that he almost felt sick.
2. Your ___condescending___ (adj.) attitude does not make people want to do what you ask.
3. They always let Cody pick the movie when they went to the theater since he considered himself a movie ___connoisseur___ (n.).
4. A squirrel had gotten into our attic, and the little ___miscreant___ (n.) chewed holes in our wiring.
5. The huge player moved ___formidably___ (adv.) down the field.

Bonus:

1. Although the professor was brilliant, he could be quite ___flighty___ (adj.) when it came to his schedule.
2. Although the Henson family was all very well behaved, they all could be guilty of ___incivility___ (adj.) when it came to who got the last cookie.

Who Said It?: Circle the correct speaker of the quote given.

1. "I'm a plain man; rum and bacon and eggs is what I want."

   a. Dr. Livesey
   b. Jim Hawkins
   (c.) The captain/Billy Bones
   d. Jim's mother
   e. Squire Trelawney
   f. the blind beggar

2. "If I can't see, I can hear a finger stirring."

   a. Dr. Livesey
   b. Jim Hawkins
   c. The captain/Billy Bones
   d. Jim's mother
   e. Squire Trelawney
   (f.) the blind beggar

3. "I'll have my dues, and not a farthing over."

   a. Dr. Livesey
   b. Jim Hawkins
   c. The captain/Billy Bones
   (d.) Jim's mother
   e. Squire Trelawney
   f. the blind beggar

4. "I believe I have the thing in my breast-pocket."

a. Dr. Livesey
(b.) Jim Hawkins
c. The captain/Billy Bones
d. Jim's mother
e. Squire Trelawney
f. the blind beggar

5. "I'll be as silent as the grave."

a. Dr. Livesey
b. Jim Hawkins
c. The captain/Billy Bones
d. Jim's mother
(e.) Squire Trelawney
f. the blind beggar

Multiple Choice: Circle the correct answer.

1. Who haunted Jim's dreams?

a. the captain/Billy Bones
(b.) the man with one leg
c. Jim's father
d. Black Dog

2. What was the captain's reaction to seeing Black Dog?

a. happy
b. sickened
c. surprised
(d.) both b and c

3. Who or what caused the death of the captain/Billy Bones?

a. Captain Flint
b. the blind beggar
c. Black Dog
(d.) the black spot

4. What did Jim's mother call the neighboring people after she asked them for help?

(a.) chicken-hearted
b. heroes
c. yellow
d. brave

5. According to Pew, who else was involved in the plot?

a. Captain Flint
b. Captain Bones
(c.) Black Dog
d. the man with one leg

6. What did Jim think the beggar and his men were looking for at the inn?

a. money
b. the black spot
(c.) Flint's fist
d. revenge on Captain Bones

7. What was in the oilskin packet?

a. gold
(b.) a treasure map
c. tobacco
d. all of the above

8. Why was the doctor hesitant to join the expedition?

(a.) He feared the squire wouldn't keep it a secret.
b. He didn't believe there was a hidden treasure.
c. He didn't want to put Jim in danger.
d. He was afraid for his own life.

Quiz 2 Answer Key

Chapters 7-11

Name ______________________________

Date ______________________________

Vocabulary: Supply the Mastery Word that makes the most sense in the sentence. Make sure to use the correct form.

brood   derisive   dexterity/dexterous   mirth   slight

1. The bully laughed ___derisively___ (adv.) at his classmate.
2. "It is not by muscle, speed, or physical ___dexterity___ (n.) that great things are achieved, but by reflection, force of character, and judgment." – Cicero
3. "Meat eaten without either ___mirth___ (n.) or music is of ill digestion." – Sir Walter Scott
4. There she sat, ___brooding___ (v.) over her lost purse.
5. The worker felt ___slighted___ (adj.) when they gave the promotion to someone else.

Bonus:

1. The stubborn child would not ___relinquish___(v.) his sister's stolen toy.
2. Defeat after defeat could not dampen the ___indomitable___ (adj.) spirit of the little league's last place team.

Who Said It?: Circle the correct speaker of the quote given.

1. "Imagine the abominable age we live in!"

a. Dr. Livesey
b. Jim Hawkins
c. Long John Silver
d. Israel Hands
(e.) Squire Trelawney
f. Captain Smollett

2. "You're as smart as paint."

a. Dr. Livesey
b. Jim Hawkins
(c.) Long John Silver
d. Israel Hands
e. Squire Trelawney
f. Captain Smollet

3. "I don't like this cruise; I don't like the men; and I don't like my officer. That's short and sweet."

a. Dr. Livesey
b. Jim Hawkins
c. Long John Silver
d. Israel Hands
e. Squire Trelawney
(f.) Captain Smollet

4. "A trifle more of that man, and I should explode."

a. Dr. Livesey
b. Jim Hawkins
c. Long John Silver
d. Israel Hands
(e.) Squire Trelawney
f. Captain Smollet

5. "Dooty is dooty, mates. I give my vote—death."

a. Dr. Livesey
b. Jim Hawkins
(c.) Long John Silver
d. Israel Hands
e. Squire Trelawney
f. Captain Smollet

Multiple Choice: Circle the correct answer.

1. What in the squire's letter did Jim think the doctor would not like?

a. The squire spent too much money on the ship.
b. The cook the squire hired only had one leg.
(c.) The squire told people in Bristol about the treasure.
d. The squire said Jim could spend only one night with his mother.

2. Why did Jim cry before leaving home?

(a.) His mother hired an apprentice boy to take Jim's place.
b. He missed his father.
c. He was afraid of leaving home on a dangerous mission.
d. He didn't get to say goodbye to his mother.

3. What was Jim's overall impression of Long John Silver after meeting him?

a. Jim was suspicious of Silver.
b. Jim was afraid of Silver.
c. Jim thought Silver was bad-tempered.
(d.) Jim felt comfortable with Silver.

4. Who did the squire call "unmanly, unsailorly, and downright un-English"?

(a.) Captain Smollett
b. Long John Silver
c. Mr. Arrow
d. Israel Hands

5. What happened to Mr. Arrow?

a. He stole the treasure map.
(b.) He disappeared.
c. He was killed by someone on board.
d. He got violently ill.

6. What did Captain Smollett admit?

a. The crew was well-behaved.
b. He still disliked the cruise.
c. He fancied the ship itself.
(d.) all of the above

7. What did Dick ask Silver about the plan?

a. He asked how much treasure he would get.
(b.) He asked what to do with the crew afterwards.
c. He asked not to be killed.
d. He asked where the treasure was.

8. Who did Silver want to kill himself?

a. Captain Smollett
b. Dr. Livesey
(c.) Squire Trelawney
d. Jim

Quiz 3 Answer Key

Chapters 12-16

Name ______________________

Date ______________________

Vocabulary: Supply the Mastery Word that makes the most sense in the sentence. Make sure to use the correct form.

duplicity   extricate   qualm

1. The magician was able to deftly ___extricate___(v.) himself from the straightjacket.
2. The longer the politician spoke, the more ___duplicitous___(adj.) his words sounded.
3. Brett had no ___qualm___(n.) with taking the last doughnut.

Bonus:

1. The teacher felt that somehow break dancing was ___incongruous___(adv.) with Latin recitation.
2. Scott thought the heat wasn't merely inconvenient, it was down-right ___abominable___(adj.).

Who Said It?: Circle the correct speaker of the quote given.

1. "And to think that they're all Englishmen! Sir, I could find it in my heart to blow the ship up."

    a. Dr. Livesey
    b. Tom
    c. Long John Silver
    d. Ben Gunn
    (e.) Squire Trelawney
    f. Captain Smollett

2. "I don't know about treasure, but I'll stake my wig there's fever here."

    (a.) Dr. Livesey
    b. Tom
    c. Long John Silver
    d. Ben Gunn
    e. Squire Trelawney
    f. Captain Smollett

3. "If I die like a dog, I'll die in my duty."

    a. Dr. Livesey
    (b.) Tom
    c. Long John Silver
    d. Ben Gunn
    e. Squire Trelawney
    f. Captain Smollett

4. "If you was sent by Long John, I'm as good as pork, and I know it."

    a. Dr. Livesey
    b. Tom
    c. Long John Silver
    (d.) Ben Gunn
    e. Squire Trelawney
    f. Captain Smollett

5. "I know you are a good man at bottom, and I daresay not one of the lot of you's as bad as he makes out."

a. Dr. Livesey
b. Tom
c. Long John Silver
d. Ben Gunn
e. Squire Trelawney
(f.) Captain Smollett

Multiple Choice: Circle the correct answer.

1. What surprised Jim most about Silver?

a. how he could move about so quickly on one leg
b. how he was planning to murder everyone to keep the treasure for himself
(c.) how cool he was while giving information about the island
d. how nice he was

2. Why did the squire, doctor, and captain feel Jim could help them more than anyone else?

a. Jim was a good liar.
(b.) The crew was open with Jim.
c. Silver trusted Jim.
d. Jim knew where to find the treasure.

3. Who was the "one man to rely on" for our heroes?

a. Jim
(b.) Long John Silver
c. Ben Gunn
d. Captain Smollett

4. What was Jim's initial emotion after escaping onto the island?

a. fear for his safety
b. relief to stretch his legs
c. regret for leaving his friends behind
(d.) joy to explore the island

5. Who was the victim of "The First Blow"?

a. Jim b. Tom c. Silver (d.) Alan

6. What did Ben Gunn want from Jim?

a. to be left alone
b. the treasure map
(c.) cheese
d. all of the above

7. According to Ben Gunn, who put him there on the island?

a. Captain Flint (b.) Providence c. Long John Silver d. the devil

8. Who among the crew did Captain Smollett risk his life for?

(a.) Abraham Gray
b. Joyce
c. Hunter
d. Dick

Quiz 4 Answer Key

Chapters 17-24

Name ______________________

Date ______________________

Vocabulary: Supply the Mastery Word that makes the most sense in the sentence. Make sure to use the correct form.

acquiesce infallible flourish callous

1. Andrew wondered how his father could be so ___callous___(adj.) as to not let him get the new video game.
2. The salesman ___flourished___(v.) at his new job.
3. After he explained his position clearly, his friend finally ___acquiesced___(v.) to the truth.
4. "The wise know too well their weakness to assume ___infallibility___(n.); and he who knows most, knows best how little he knows." - Thomas Jefferson

Bonus:

1. The angry prisoner hurled ___imprecations___ (n.) at his jailers.
2. Tanya found it difficult to ___ascertain___ (v.) her son's motive when he brought her candy.

Who Said It?: Circle the correct speaker of the quote given.

1. "Strike my colors! No, sir, not I."

   a. Abraham Gray
   b. Jim Hawkins
   c. Long John Silver
   d. Ben Gunn
   e. Squire Trelawney
   (f.) Captain Smollett

2. "You're a good boy, or I'm mistook; but you're only a boy, all told."

   a. Abraham Gray
   b. Jim Hawkins
   c. Long John Silver
   (d.) Ben Gunn
   e. Squire Trelawney
   f. Captain Smollett

3. "Laugh, by thunder, laugh! Before an hour's out, ye'll laugh upon the other side. Them that die'll be the lucky ones."

   a. Abraham Gray
   b. Jim Hawkins
   (c.) Long John Silver
   d. Ben Gunn
   e. Squire Trelawney
   f. Captain Smollett

4. "Well, shipmate, mad he may not be; but if *he's* not, you mark my words, *I* am!"

(a.) Abraham Gray
b. Jim Hawkins
c. Long John Silver
d. Ben Gunn
e. Squire Trelawney
f. Captain Smollett

5. "Clumsy fellows, they must still be drunk as owls."

a. Abraham Gray
(b.) Jim Hawkins
c. Long John Silver
d. Ben Gunn
e. Squire Trelawney
f. Captain Smollett

Multiple Choice: Circle the correct answer.

1. Who was the first of Captain Smollett's men to die?

a. Hunter
b. Joyce
(c.) Redruth
d. Gray

2. What did Captain Smollett insist on doing?

(a.) hanging the British flag
b. hanging the Jolly Roger
c. searching for Jim
d. burying their man

3. What was the group's "best hope" for survival?

a. finding the treasure
(b.) killing all the mutineers
c. sending Ben Gunn as a messenger
d. hiding in the woods

4. What did Captain Smollett do when Silver came to seek a truce?

a. He handed over a fake treasure map.
(b.) He told Silver he'd take his men back to England for a fair trial.
c. He offered to give the mutineers all their provisions.
d. He shot one of Silver's men.

5. What was the price of the heroes' victory?

(a.) Joyce died.
b. Hunter died.
c. Jim was taken hostage.
d. They lost all their provisions.

6. Where did Jim think the doctor was going when he left camp?

a. to find the treasure
b. to talk to Silver
(c.) to see Ben Gunn
d. to find the Hispaniola

7. What was Jim's plan?

a. kill Silver in his sleep
(b.) cut the Hispaniola adrift
c. find Ben Gunn
d. steal back their provisions

8. How did Jim react to his impending doom in the coracle?

a. He began to cry.
b. He jumped overboard.
c. He cried out for help.
(d.) He was resigned to his death.

Quiz 5 Answer Key

Chapters 25-29

Name ______________________

Date ______________________

Vocabulary:

Supply the Mastery Word that makes the most sense in the sentence. Make sure to use the correct form.

volition dilapidate incense

1. The boys all dared each other to go into the old, ___dilapidated___ (adj.) house.
2. It does no good to simply exercise ___volition___ (n.); you need to make sure you do what is right.
3. The baby was ___incensed___ (v.) by the loss of the toy.

Bonus: truculent

1. "Remember that there is nothing stable in human affairs; therefore avoid undue ___elation___ (n.) in prosperity, or undue depression in adversity." – Socrates
2. The ___truculent___ (adj.) crowd demanded that the gold be returned to them.

Who Said It?:

Circle the correct speaker of the quote given.

1. "I don't have no manner of luck, you see, and that's what's the matter with me."

   a. George Merry
   b. Jim Hawkins
   c. Long John Silver
   (d.) Israel Hands
   e. Squire Trelawney
   f. Captain Smollett

2. "You can kill the body, Mr. Hands, but not the spirit; you must know that already."

   a. George Merry
   (b.) Jim Hawkins
   c. Long John Silver
   d. Israel Hands
   e. Squire Trelawney
   f. Captain Smollett

3. "Pieces of eight! pieces of eight!"

   a. George Merry
   (b.) Silver's parrot
   c. Long John Silver
   d. Israel Hands
   e. Job Anderson
   f. Morgan

4. "The laugh's on my side; I've had the top of this business from the first."

   a. George Merry
   (b.) Jim Hawkins
   c. Long John Silver
   d. Israel Hands
   e. Squire Trelawney
   f. Captain Smollett

5. "The black spot! I thought so."

   a. George Merry
   b. Jim Hawkins
   (c.) Long John Silver
   d. Israel Hands
   e. Squire Trelawney
   f. Captain Smollett

Multiple Choice: Circle the correct answer.

1. What did the coxswain do for Jim in exchange for food, drink, and a bandaged leg?

   a. He promised not to kill Jim.
   b. He promised to share the treasure.
   (c.) He showed Jim how to sail.
   d. He agreed to join Jim and his men.

2. How did Jim find out that the coxswain was planning to kill him?

   a. The coxswain told him this plan.
   (b.) Jim saw him hide a knife in his coat.
   c. Jim overheard him tell a crew mate.
   d. The coxswain was not planning to kill Jim.

3. What weakness in Jim was almost his downfall?

   (a.) cockiness
   b. fear
   c. suspicion
   d. his physical inferiority

4. As Jim neared the camp, what put him at ease?

   a. the sight of the camp fire
   b. the sound of Silver's parrot
   c. the smell of food cooking
   (d.) the sound of his friends snoring

5. How did Jim respond when Silver asked him to choose a side?

   a. Jim demanded to know where his friends were.
   b. Jim cried and begged Silver to spare his life.
   c. Jim said he would not defend Silver in court.
   (d.) Jim admitted to everything he'd done since overhearing them in the apple barrel.

6. What did Silver reveal to Jim was in his possession?

   (a.) the treasure map
   b. the treasure
   c. Ben Gunn
   d. the Hispaniola

7. What did the buccaneers bring back to Silver?

   a. food
   b. weapons
   (c.) the black spot
   d. the Hispaniola

8. As Jim fell asleep, for whom did he feel sorry?

   (a.) Silver
   b. himself
   c. Israel Hands
   d. Ben Gunn

Final Exam Answer Key

Chapters 1-34

Name ______________________

Date ______________________

Vocabulary: Supply the Mastery Word that makes the most sense in the sentence.

Make sure to use the correct form. Use the words in the first list to answer questions 1-8 and the second list for 9-15.

acquiesce	derelict	dilapidate	extricate
incense	qualm	rudiment	volition

1. The employee was fired because he was constantly ___derelict___ (adj.) in his duty.
2. A ___rudimentary___ (adj.) understanding of physics is needed to build a catapult.
3. After many months of deliberation, the two parties finally ___acquiesced___ (v.) to the plan suggested by the representative.
4. Her parents were surprised to see that she made her bed of her own ___volition___ (n.).
5. The Greek was ___incensed___ (v.) by the enemy's mistreatment of the temple of Athena, and he called down imprecations against them.
6. Years of misuse had left the bridge ___dilapidated___ (adj.) and not safe to cross.
7. Uncomfortable with large groups of people, he sought to ___extricate___ (v.) himself from the crowd.
8. Paris believed that Helen rightfully belonged to him, so he had no ___qualms___ (n.) about stealing her from Menelaus.

callous	duplicity	flourish	formidable
grapple	infallible	mirth	

9. The student won the debate by his ___infallible___ (adj.) use of logic.
10. The garden ___flourished___ (v.) under her attentive care.
11. When they got to the base of the mountain, the idea of climbing it seemed far more ___formidable___ (adj.) than it did the day before.
12. "You may have all the solemnity you wish in your neckties, but in anything important you must have ___mirth___ (n.) or you will have madness." - G. K. Chesterton
13. The boy cried "wolf!" so many times that the townspeople had grown ___callous___ (adj.) to his cries.
14. When she came home with her driver's permit, her parents were forced to ___grapple___ (v.) with the idea that their little girl was growing up.
15. The honest and true judge was never guilty of ___duplicity___ (n.).

Who Said It?: Circle the correct speaker of the quote given.

1. "There is a kind of fate in this."

   (a.) Dr. Livesey
   b. Jim Hawkins
   c. Long John Silver
   d. George Merry
   e. Squire Trelawney
   f. Captain Smollett

2. "We'll save our necks in spite of fate and fortune."

   a. Dr. Livesey
   b. Jim Hawkins
   (c.) Long John Silver
   d. George Merry
   e. Squire Trelawney
   f. Captain Smollett

3. "Fetch aft the rum, Darby!"

   a. Dr. Livesey
   b. Silver's parrot
   c. Long John Silver
   d. George Merry
   e. the ghost of Captain Flint
   (f.) Ben Gunn

4. "But the dead men, sir, hang about your neck like millstones."

   a. Dr. Livesey
   b. Jim Hawkins
   c. Long John Silver
   d. George Merry
   (e.) Squire Trelawney
   f. Captain Smollett

5. "You're the man to keep your word, we know that."

   (a.) Dr. Livesey
   b. Jim Hawkins
   c. Long John Silver
   d. George Merry
   e. Squire Trelawney
   f. Captain Smollett

6. "I'll be as silent as the grave."

   a. Dr. Livesey
   b. Jim Hawkins
   c. The captain/Billy Bones
   d. Jim's mother
   (e.) Squire Trelawney
   f. Pew/the blind beggar

7. "You're as smart as paint."

   a. Dr. Livesey
   b. Jim Hawkins
   (c.) Long John Silver
   d. Israel Hands
   e. Squire Trelawney
   f. Captain Smollet

8. "I know you are a good man at bottom, and I daresay not one of the lot of you's as bad as he makes out."

   a. Dr. Livesey
   b. Tom
   c. Long John Silver
   d. Ben Gunn
   e. Squire Trelawney
   (f.) Captain Smollett

9. "Strike my colors! No, sir, not I."

   a. Abraham Gray
   b. Jim Hawkins
   c. Long John Silver
   d. Ben Gunn
   e. Squire Trelawney
   (f.) Captain Smollett

10. "The laugh's on my side; I've had the top of this business from the first."

a. George Merry
(b.) Jim Hawkins
c. Long John Silver
d. Israel Hands
e. Squire Trelawney
f. Captain Smollett

Multiple Choice: Circle the correct answer.

1. Who or what caused the death of the captain/Billy Bones?

a. Captain Flint
b. the blind beggar
c. Black Dog
(d.) the black spot

2. What did Jim think the beggar and his men were looking for at the inn?

a. money
b. the black spot
(c.) Flint's fist
d. revenge on Captain Bones

3. What was Jim's overall impression of Long John Silver after meeting him?

a. Jim was suspicious of Silver.
b. Jim was afraid of Silver.
c. Jim thought Silver was bad-tempered.
(d.) Jim felt comfortable with Silver.

4. Who did the squire initially loathe?

(a.) Captain Smollett
b. Long John Silver
c. Mr. Arrow
d. Israel Hands

5. Why did the squire, doctor, and captain feel Jim could help them more than anyone else?

a. Jim was a good liar.
(b.) The crew was open with Jim.
c. Silver trusted Jim.
d. Jim knew where to find the treasure.

6. Who was the victim of "The First Blow"?

a. Jim
b. Tom
c. Silver
(d.) Alan

7. What did Captain Smollett insist on doing?

(a.) hanging the British flag
b. hanging the Jolly Roger
c. searching for Jim
d. burying their man

8. What was the group's "best hope" for survival?

a. finding the treasure
(b.) killing all the mutineers
c. sending Ben Gunn as a messenger
d. hiding in the woods

9. How did Jim find out that the coxswain was planning to kill him?

a. The coxswain told him this plan.
(b.) Jim saw him hide a knife in his coat.
c. Jim overheard him tell a crew mate.
d. The coxswain was not planning to kill Jim.

10. What weakness in Jim was almost his downfall against Israel Hands?

(a.) cockiness
b. fear
c. suspicion
d. his physical inferiority

11. What was Flint's pointer?

a. a very tall tree
(b.) a pirate's skeleton
c. a pickaxe
d. a pointy rock

12. What were Captain Flint's last words?

a. "Darby M'Graw!"
b. "Pieces of eight! pieces of eight!"
c. "Shiver me timbers!"
(d.) "Fetch aft the rum, Darby!"

13. Whose was the voice the pirates heard?

(a.) Ben Gunn
b. Jim
c. Captain Flint
d. Dr. Livesey

14. What became of Silver?

a. He was left on the island to die.
b. He jumped overboard on the trip back.
c. He was hanged on the gallows.
(d.) He escaped with a sack of coins.

15. Who wasted his share of the treasure?

a. Jim
b. Squire Trelawney
(c.) Ben Gunn
d. Captain Smollett

Characters: Match the following characters with their correct description.

1. O Jim Hawkins
2. L Captain Smollett
3. E Dr. Livesey
4. G Squire Trelawney
5. J Long John Silver
6. K Israel Hands
7. D Tom Morgan
8. C Black Dog
9. A Billy Bones
10. F Mr. Arrow
11. H Tom Redruth
12. P George Merry
13. B Pew
14. N Captain Flint
15. I Ben Gunn
16. M Abraham Gray

A. old pirate with a scar on his cheek; given the black spot
B. blind beggar; delivered the black spot
C. pirate missing two fingers; visited the Admiral Benbow Inn
D. seen drinking at the Spy-glass tavern; wanted to kill Jim
E. narrated part of the story; gave treatment to sick men
F. the ship's mate; a drunk; disappeared one night
G. landowner who financed the treasure hunt expedition
H. the gamekeeper; the first casualty of our heroes
I. maroon living on the island for three years
J. the ship's cook; double-dealing one-legged pirate
K. the ship's coxswain; Jim killed him
L. captain of the ship; became quite a hero
M. originally a mutineer; joined the captain and his men
N. infamous pirate; buried treasure on an island
O. narrator of most of the story; young boy
P. buccaneer with yellow eyes; accused Silver of ruining the trip

Essay: Answer the following question on the lines provided.

Who do you think was the greatest hero of *Treasure Island*: Jim Hawkins, Captain Smollett, Ben Gunn, or someone else? Give detailed evidence from the book to support your choice.